GW00372883

COLLINS GEM
BASIC FACTS

COMPUTERS

Brian Samways BSc

Revised by
Peter Robinson BA

COLLINS
London and Glasgow

First published 1983
Revised edition 1988
Reprint 10 9 8 7 6 5 4 3 2

© William Collins Sons & Co. Ltd 1988

ISBN 0 00 459105 4
ISBN 0 00 459271 9

Printed in Great Britain

Introduction

Basic Facts is a new generation of illustrated GEM dictionaries in important school subjects. They cover all the main ideas and topics in these subjects up to the level of first examinations.

Bold words in an entry mean a word or idea is developed further in a separate entry; *italic* words are highlighted for importance.

There is a list of useful abbreviations and acronyms at the end of the dictionary.

Abacus One of the first gadgets for doing arithmetic, used for addition and subtraction. It has ten balls or beads in each row if working in **denary**. Multiplication and division are carried out by repeated addition and subtraction, just as in calculators and computers today. Another similarity is that it stores the result as well as doing the calculation. An advanced type is still used in parts of China as a cheap, easy-to-use calculating device and is very fast in the hands of an expert.

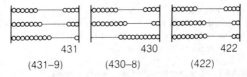

| | 431 | 430 | 422 |
| | (431−9) | (430−8) | (422) |

For example: to calculate 431−9, note that ten beads on one row can be exchanged for one ball on the row above at any time during a calculation.

Abort In the same way as the countdown of a space launch is sometimes stopped, so the running of a computer program is made to cease when things go wrong. In both cases we use the word abort, though in the computer case it returns to the **operating system**

1

after aborting the program. The computer then prints a message and waits for a command.

Absolute Address   To visit a friend you need to find the house, and you can do this if you have the address. **Data** held in a computer is found by giving the address of its location. When we program in a **low-level language** the number given to each address is governed by the **hardware** and is called the absolute address.

Access Time   The time taken by the computer to fetch **data** from an **address** within the computer or other storage device. The time between being told to fetch and having the data ready.

ACE   See **Automatic Computing Engine**.

Accumulator   A special **location** used to perform calculations when doing arithmetic. The accumulator, on being given a number, can add it to the number already held and then hold the result. It also transfers data back to the central memory or outputs it to peripherals.

For example, a program in **machine code** designed to add two numbers together would carry out the arithmetic with three instructions:

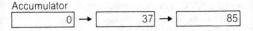

Accumulator

| 0 | → | 37 | → | 85 |

a) clear accumulator
b) transfer first number to accumulator (37)
c) add second number to accumulator (48)

Acoustic Coupler A communications device into which a telephone handset can be fitted. Digital signals using **serial transmission** can then be sent from or to a computer via the telephone system. Two tones (i.e. two different sounds) are used, one for 0's and one for 1's.

mains lead

to computer

Acronym The world of computing has many acronyms. These consist of a simple set of letters taken from the letters of a word or phrase. For example, the

3

word **BASIC** is an acronym made from 'Beginners' **A**ll-purpose **S**ymbolic **I**nstruction **C**ode' but it is much easier to say 'BASIC'.

There is a list of acronyms at the end of this book.

ADA   A **high-level** programming language used in military and other systems. It is named after Ada, Lady Lovelace (1815-52), daughter of Lord Byron and a mathematician who was assistant to Charles **Babbage**.

ADC   See **A to D**.

Adder   A device which performs addition on digital signals giving both the sum and the carry digit. A **half-adder** has two inputs each of which can be a 0 or 1 whereas a full-adder has three inputs.

For example, when adding two binary numbers together electronically the first column on the right can be dealt with by a **half-adder** but the other columns require a full-adder as there is a carry digit from the previous column.

$$\begin{array}{r}
1001101 \\
+0110111 \\
\hline
10000100
\end{array}$$

Address A computer stores **data**, and so that it can be found each store-**location** has an address.

For example, address 142 holds the letter T, though both would be stored in **binary notation**. Just as the word CAT is held in three locations so more than one location can be used to hold a number.

address	contents
140	C
141	A
142	T
143	255

Address Bus A major route (set of wires) along which signals travel to indicate a particular **address**. **Data** can then be put into or taken from that address along the data **bus**.

Address Modification This is a process by which the address part of a program instruction is changed, say to one higher (i.e. the next address) each time the instruction is performed. This is very useful if a series of inputs are to be placed in consecutive addresses.

Aiken Howard Aiken, an American, realized the importance of Babbage's **analytical engine** and suggested the Automatic Sequence Controlled Calculator (ASCC) which, built in the mid-1940s, was the first automatic computer. The program instructions were supplied to this electromechanical machine on paper tape.

ALGOL (acronym for ALGorithmic Oriented Language) a high-level programming language developed in Europe at the same time as **FORTRAN** was being developed in the United States. ALGOL60 is a problem-solving language designed for mathematical and scientific use whereas ALGOL 68 is an even more powerful language designed in 1968 for a variety of uses.

Algorithm A planned set of instructions or steps designed to solve a particular problem. There is only one starting point and all routes through the algorithm end at the same finishing point. Such steps can be carried out by a computer, or dry run on paper, using different inputs or values.

Algorithmic Oriented Language See **ALGOL**.

Allocate See **Assign**.

Alphabetical Order The order of the letters of the alphabet from A to Z. Computers do not always

follow strict alphabetical order when sorting because
ASCII codes list all capital letters before lowercase
letters. For example, 'Z' (code 90) comes before 'a'
(code 97). Some computers have separate codes
which allow the capital and lowercase versions of a
letter to come together.

Alphanumeric Code A set of characters consisting of the letters A to Z and numbers 0 to 9.
 For example: an alphanumeric keyboard.

(1) (2) (3) (4) (5) (6) (7) (8) (9) (0)
 (Q) (W) (E) (R) (T) (Y) (U) (I) (O) (P)
  (A) (S) (D) (F) (G) (H) (J) (K) (L)
   (Z) (X) (C) (V) (B) (N) (M)

ALU See **Arithmetic Logic Unit**.

Amplifier A device that accepts a varying electrical signal and is capable of making its voltage (or the
current) bigger.

Analogue Computer This is a machine designed
to work on **data** which is represented by some physical
quantity which varies continuously (unlike digital signals which are 0's and 1's).

For example: the turning of a wheel or changes in voltage can be used as input. Analogue computers are said to operate in **real time** because they respond as things happen and are widely used for research in design where many different shapes and speeds can be tried out quickly. A computer model of a car suspension allows the designer to see the effects of changing size, stiffness and damping.

Analogue-Digital Converter   See **A to D Converter**.

Analytical Engine   The first machine designed to carry out complicated arithmetical tasks. Invented in 1833 by the Englishman Charles **Babbage** it was ahead of its time as the engineers could not make all the necessary parts to the required accuracy. The mechanical forerunner of today's computer.

Ancestral File   See **Backup**.

AND Gate   This is a logic gate which operates with **binary digits**. Its output is of logic value 1 only when all its inputs have a logic value 1.

For example: with a two input AND gate the following **truth table** applies:

an AND gate

Input		Output
0	0	0
0	1	0
1	0	0
1	1	1

This could be used to find the carry digit when two binary digits are added together as there is a carry of 1 only when the two digits to be added are both 1's.

APL Acronym for A Programming Language, a language designed originally for IBM mainframe computers and now not often found.

Applications Package The name given to a program or set of programs, with user manuals and documentation, written to carry out a specific task. For example: a wages payroll package, a warehouse-control program, or a program controlling a robot welder.

9

Application Specific Integrated Circuits (ASICS) See **ASICS**.

Archived File As the name suggests this type of file is kept, say, on magnetic tape and has to be loaded on to the disk or tape drive when required. It is not kept permanently in the computer and so does not take up valuable space.

Argument A variable factor, the value of which sets the value of the function of which it is part.

For example: to find the square root when programming in **BASIC** we use a function such as SQR(X). The value of this function is governed by the value of the argument X.

Arithmetic Logic Unit (ALU) This is the part of

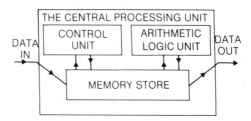

the computer where the calculations are carried out (addition and substraction) and the logic operations are performed. The ALU is part of the **central processing unit** and has an arithmetic register for holding the results of calculations while processing is going on.

Array The name given to an arranged set of locations any of which can be accessed from a common starting address, or identifier, rather than individually.

For example: consider a block of flats having eight floors with four flats on each floor. The flats could be numbered (coded) 1 to 32 as in a one-dimensional array and referred to as FLAT 1, FLAT 2 etc. Alternatively they could be numbered 11 to 14 on the first level, 21 to 24 on the second level, 31 to 34 on the third level as in a two-dimensional array and referred to as LEVEL 2 ROOM 3 etc. (Note that when using rows and columns an item of **data** is always accessed by the row and then the column). If the names of the people who live in the flats are Oakley, Talbot, Thomas, Foster, Fish, Simmons, Selby, Ellis, Nelson and so on, then these names could be stored in a one-dimensional array F$1, F$2, F$3, etc. (In **BASIC** the $ signifies a **string**):

F\$(1)	Oakley
F\$(2)	Talbot
F\$(3)	Thomas
F\$(4)	Foster
F\$(5)	Fish

However a two-dimensional array is more convenient when dealing with large amounts of **data**:

1st level	Oakley	Talbot	Thomas	Foster
2nd level	Fish	Simons	Selby	Ellis

To obtain the names of those living at the seventh level we would use references F\$(7,1), F\$(7,2), F\$(7,3) and F\$(7,4).

Artificial Intelligence This is the name used to describe software which teaches the computer how to learn from its experiences and to make decisions based on these experiences, rather like a human being.

For example: a machine may play chess, but if each time it plays it learns from its mistakes and plays better the next time, then it is said to have artificial intelligence.

ASCC (Automatic Sequence Controlled Computer) See **Aiken**.

ASCII Code (acronymn for American Standard Code for Information Interchange — pronounced 'ASKEY') A standard code used for the transmission of **data**, particularly the exchange of data between machines. Many manufacturers design their own codes for their machines but ASCII code is often used as a standard thus enabling link-ups between various computers and **peripherals** such as **printers**:

0	48	C	67	O	79	a	97
1	49	D	68	P	80	b	98
2	50	E	69	Q	81	c	99
3	51	F	70	R	82	d	100
4	52	G	71	S	83	e	101
5	53	H	72	T	84	space	32
6	54	I	73	U	85	!	33
7	55	J	74	V	86	*	42
8	56	K	75	W	87	+	43
9	57	L	76	X	88	−	45
A	65	M	77	Y	89	/	47
B	66	N	78	Z	90	=	61

ASICS (Application Specific Integrated Circuits) The development of customized chips for manufacturers of other products. Sometimes called 'dedicated chips', these may be used for controlling a particular task, for example, washing-machine programs, speech recognition chips, the operation of modern hifi equipment.

The greatly increased popularity of ASICS has been brought about by new design and manufacturing methods based on standardized chip-building blocks rather than designing from scratch, which has enabled the costs of development to be reduced.

Aspect Ratio   The ratio of the width of a television screen to the height. 4:3 has been adopted by the United Kingdom and many other countries.

Assembler   The program that translates **assembly language** into machine code.

Assembly Language   This is a **low-level language** which is similar to the way in which the computer hardware works but is easier to use than machine code for programming. The computer manufacturer provides an *assembler* and this program translates the completed assembly language program into **machine code**, one programming instruction becoming one machine code instruction.

Assign   This is reserving part of the computing

system, say the printer, for use by a program during its running. Note that *allocate* is similar but is controlled during the running and may make the particular hardware available to other programs at certain times.

Astable   The adjective used for an electronic device which has two states but is continually switching (oscillating) from one to the other. It is used as the timing device in electronic watches and as the basis for the computer **clock**.

Asynchronous Mode   The way in which a computer works whereby the end of one operation allows the start of the next. The machine does not have to wait for the next **clock** cycle to start each operation, as in **synchronous mode**.

Atlas   The best-known of the **second generation** computers which were built using **transistors** as opposed to the thermionic **valves** of the **first generation**.

ATM (Automated Telling Machine)   A computerized cash dispenser which accepts cash-cards.

A to D Converter (analogue to digital) A device that is able to convert a continuously varying signal, such as voltage, into a series of numbers. It does this by sampling the voltage at regular intervals (ten times a second say) and changing its digital output accordingly.

For example: when a computer is used to switch on and off a heating system it must be able to measure the temperature. Electrical thermometers provide varying voltages (analogue) which have to be converted into a series of digits (a binary number) for the computer.

Audit Trail   See **Lasercard**.

Author Language The name given to a programming language that allows the user to have little or no knowledge of programming. With an author language the non-computer specialist can compose a learning sequence in a particular subject for his own students.

For example: **PILOT** is an author language specially developed for **computer-assisted learning** packages.

Automated Telling Machine   See **ATM**.

Automatic Computing Engine (ACE) The fastest of the early computers built in 1950 by the National Physics Laboratory. Parts can still be seen in the London Science Museum.

Automatic Sequence Controlled Computer (ASCC) See **Aiken**.

Auto-start With some commercial micro-computers an auto-start code is stored in **read-only-memory (ROM)**. In such cases on switching on this automatically loads, say, the **BASIC interpreter** and a program into the machine which is then immediately ready for use.

Babbage   Charles Babbage (1791-1871) was an English mathematician who saw the need for an accurate calculating device and tried to build a 'difference engine'. In 1833 he proposed the **analytical engine** which in principle was the fore-runner of today's computer. Using punched cards it was designed to perform calculations automatically and was the first type of digital computer.

Backing Store   A store for large amounts of **data** which can be transmitted easily (though not always quickly) to the **main store** when required. It also has the advantage of being a non-**volatile memory**.

  For example: magnetic card or magnetic disk.

Backup   Designed to provide a service when things go wrong. Also, should a set of records become corrupt then this allows one to start again with the original **data**.

  For example: in keeping records on a **disk** for a **microcomputer** one should keep three copies. These are called *ancestral files*. Should one disk become damaged during updating, the operator can continue with the next copy knowing that there is still a third copy. If there were only two copies and the first was damaged, then the second has to be duplicated on to another disk before being **updated** and this could result in the updated records being lost whilst the second disk is being copied. The third copy is always stored separately from the first two.

Bar Code These consist of a set of lines of varying widths which can be read by passing a **light pen** across them. On household goods there are 30 lines giving a unique 13-digit code number to each product. On being recorded by the cashier, the machine finds the price from **memory** and is able to record the fact that there is now one less of that item in stock.

Library cards and library books sometimes have bar codes, though with more lines. Here the borrowing of books during the day is recorded on to tape using a light pen and the **data** transferred to the computer at the end of the day.

BASIC (acronym for Beginner's All-purpose

Symbolic Instruction Code) **A high-level language** used for general or conversational programming. Developed by Kemeny and Kurtz in 1964 in the USA, it was originally designed for educational use as an easy-to-learn language. Students could input their programs one line at a time, each of which would be checked by the computer before the next one would be accepted.

Batch Processing The system of collecting all the different inputs or **programs** together and putting them into a computer in one set or a batch. This only involves the operator in 'one' loading and running operation no matter how many programs are in the batch. The programs are processed as a single unit thus avoiding wasted computer time as each program is loaded. Job control cards control each program while it is processed.

For example: in a school without its own computing facilities each pupil in a class could write a program on **mark sense cards** which can be taken and fed, on batch, to a distant computer. Not only would there usually be a delay before these could be run but several days could pass before the output is returned.

Batch Total See **Hash Total**.

Baud Rate Named after the French inventor J.M.E. Baudot (1845-1903), this rate today is taken as the number of **bits** per second transmitted along a wire. Originally it was based on the speeds of transmitting the morse code.

Rate	Used by
110 baud	Teletype terminal to computer
300 baud	Slow-speed cassette tape to micro
1200 baud	Prestel set receiving data
7000000 baud	Data transfer by satellites
1000 million baud	Possible speed with optic fibre

BCS Abbreviation for the British Computer Society.

BCD See **Binary Coded Decimal**.

Beginner's All-purpose Symbolic Instruction Code See **BASIC**.

Benchmark A program task which is given to different makes of computers to measure their performance thus enabling a comparison to be made.

Binary Coded Decimal (BCD) To be able to change any of our numbers 0 to 9 into binary, we require up to four **binary digits**. The coding system BCD uses four binary digits for each decimal number.

decimal	binary code
0	0000
1	0001
2	0010
3	0011
4	0100
5	0101
6	0110
7	0111
8	1000
9	1001

denary	binary	hex
10	1010	A
11	1011	B
12	1100	C
13	1101	D
14	1110	E
15	1111	F

But note that with four binary digits numbers up to 15

can be coded in this way. The final six numbers are coded as letters in the **hexadecimal** system.

Binary Digit   Either a 0 or 1. It is one of the two digits used in **binary notation**.

Binary Fractions   Each **binary digit** has twice the value of the one on its right whether it comes before or after the bicimal point.

For example: 11.11 in binary represents $2+1+\frac{1}{2}+\frac{1}{4}=3.75$ in **denary**.

Binary Notation   In this system numbers are represented by the two digits 0 and 1, i.e. base 2.

Binary	Denary
0	0
1	1
10	2
11	3
100	4

Binary	Denary
101	5
110	6
111	7
1000	8

and so on.

When we count in tens (base 10) each digit is ten times the value of the one on its right. In binary (base 2) each digit has twice the value.

For example: 10011 in binary is 19 in denary:

16	8	4	2	1
1	0	0	1	1

$$16+0+0+2+1=19$$

Using the same rules as for denary arithmetic:

binary addition	binary subtraction
0010	1101
+1011	−0110
1101	0111

Binary notation having only two digits can be easily represented electronically by two voltage levels and can be stored in any system having two states. For these reasons it is used by computers.

Bistable The adjective used for an electronic device which has two states and is the basis of a computer memory. In one state it can be considered to represent a 0 and in the other state a 1.

Bit One of the two digits 0 and 1 used in **binary notation**. The word comes from BInary digiT.

Black Box A concept used to understand how units go together to make a system without having to understand the workings of the individual units.

For example: a public address system may be considered to be just three black boxes:

and the amplifier itself as three black boxes:

BLAISE Acronym for the British Library Automated Information Service.

Block A set of records, figures or words which are treated by the computer as a single unit of **data**.

For example: **microcomputer** data is transferred to and from a cassette tape recorder in blocks. These blocks are sometimes indicated by numbers on the screen though they can be distinctly heard by just playing the tape.

Block Diagram This is a diagram used to help explain a system and consists of labelled boxes joined by lines with arrows similar to a program **flowchart**. It is used for systems such as electrical circuits.

For example:

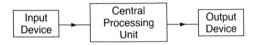

Boolean Algebra First presented to the world in 1847 by the English mathematician George Boole (1815-64) this set of rules allows logical statements to be written using algebra. The results of such statements can be shown in a **truth table**.

Bootstrap The loading of a program into a computer, say by pressing a certain key, which first calls in routines which have to be used to load programs. Switching on a computer does not mean that it is ready — 'booting' the system normally gives the user some form of **operating system**.

Branch A computer carries out each program step in turn but can be made to jump to a different part of the program by a branch instruction.

For example: a conditional branch might depend on the value of something at that time, i.e. branch if the

26

value of X is greater than 7. **Structured programming** avoids the use of the branch.

Breadboard An experimental circuit board which is used to try out possible circuits. Often included on a **microprocessor** learning/teaching kit for **interfacing** and control technology.

Broadband A transmission technique which uses a wide range of frequencies to allow telecommunications messages to be sent simultaneously. See also **Data Communications**.

BSI Abbreviation for British Standards Institution, the body which sets and maintains standards for units of measurement, technical terminology, etc., in Britain.

Bubble Memory Used for storing **data** in **binary notation**. Small cylinders of magnetism, called bubbles, are created and held stationary by magnets in an **integrated circuit** (or **chip**) made from magnetic material. Each bubble is used to represent a 1 whereas the absence of a bubble indicates a 0.

To keep the bubbles in place chevrons are put on the

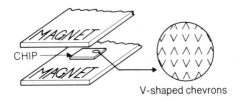

V-shaped chevrons

surface of the chip (shown V-shaped in the inset diagram). Bubbles are created at one end, moved by magnetic fields (not shown in diagram) across the chip as required and read in sequence. Thus it is a **serial access memory** but has the advantage of being non-**volatile** and capable of high density storage. This whole book could be stored as 0's and 1's on four bubble memory chips each less than a square centimetre.

Buffer A temporary store for data which is being transferred, generally used to allow for a difference in speeds.

For example: what is typed on a **microcomputer** keyboard is generally held in a buffer until the return or input key is pressed. Many **printers** have buffers that are filled with what is to be printed at a much faster rate than the actual printing.

Bug A mistake in a program or an error in the working of the computer. Bugs can be removed by running **diagnostic routines** to discover the error and then by **debugging**.

Bus A route around the computer consisting of a set of wires along which signals travel in parallel. These signals can start from any place on the bus and can travel to any destination.

For example: in a microcomputer the **address bus** would carry signals to select a particular storage location; the **data bus** may then carry signals to transfer data to that location.

Byte A name given to a set of eight **binary digits**, usually representing one **character**, which is treated by the computer as one unit. (Any set of binary digits treated as a working unit is called a **word**.) For example, some computers use 32-**bit** words make up of various groupings, for instance two groups of 16 bits. In the case of 18-bit words, each of the characters could be coded using six binary digits. Letter A might be 100001, C might be 100011 and T 110100. Thus a three-character message would be coded as:

100011100001110100

and this is treated as an 18-bit word. Larger messages require more than one word. In this case 6 bits make 1 byte and 3 bytes make one word.

C A **high-level language** widely used by professionals for operating systems, games and business software.

CAA Abbreviation for Computer-Aided Administration.

CAD Acronym for Computer-Aided Design, a **program** which can convert a designer's or artist's rough sketches into a more finished form, using devices such as a mouse or a wand.

CAL See **Computer-Assisted Learning**.

Calculator A machine which is able to do arithmetic (add, subtract, multiply and divide) and other logical operations. A programmable calculator is one which carries out a set of arithmetical operations in order according to a program. Even early calculators that worked with **punched cards** were able to follow simple programs, although they were not able to change their own programs or to do repeated loops and branching.

CAM Acronym for Computer-Aided Manufacture.

31

Card Punch A machine that punches holes in cards so that the cards store data which can be used at a later time. When **on line** the holes are punched by signals from the computer (300 cards per minute say): **off line** they are punched by hand.

Card Reader This machine reads cards which have been prepared by the **card punch**. The data stored on the cards is taken and put in another form (e.g. electrical signals) which can be used by a computer or other device. Reading speeds of over 1000 cards per minute are possible.

Cassette Tape A cheap form of **backup** storage used with **microcomputers**. It has the advantage of being readily available (same as that used in cassette tape recorders) but is somewhat slow (between 300 and 1200 **baud**) in transferring **data**. Note that most microcomputer programs can be stored on one side of a ten-minute tape; i.e. a C10 tape.

CBT (Computer Based Training) See **Computer-Assisted Learning**.

CCITT Abbreviation for Consultative Committee

International Telegraph and Telephone, the organization which standardizes international **data communications**.

CD-I (Compact Disc Interactive)   See **Compact Disc**.

CD-ROM (Compact Disc Read Only Memory)
See **Compact Disc**.

Ceefax   The name of the BBC's **teletext** service which transmits **data** along with the normal programme transmissions. With a teletext decoder this data can be made to fill the screen (or be superimposed over the picture) one page at a time. The **data** from page 700 onwards when loaded into particular **microcomputers** provides **software** for those machines. Software transmitted thus is called **telesoftware**.

Central Processing Unit (CPU)   The brains or nerve centre of a computer. It has three parts: its own **store**, an **arithmetic logic unit** and a **control unit**. The control unit carries out each instruction of a program in turn. This may involve arithmetic operations being carried out on **data** being held or the moving of data from one part of the computer to another. The central processing unit is sometimes known as the *central processor.*

Character Any keyboard symbol. It can be a digit (0,1,2 . . .), a letter (A,B,C, . . .), a punctuation mark (!,',?, . . .), a sign (⋆,+,−, . . .) or just a space.

Character Code The binary code used by computers to represent **characters**. Each machine often has its own character code though there are some standard codes like **ASCII**.

Character Recognition Whereas computers can understand dots and punched holes, humans can read **characters**. To input characters into a computer one can use a keyboard to provide **character codes** though it would be much quicker if the computer could recognize written or printed characters. **Optical character recognition** (OCR) and **magnetic ink** character recognition (MICR) are the two main systems of automatically recognizing characters.

Chart Recorder A record-keeping device that

plots graphs by the movement of a pen to the right or left as a piece of paper is moved steadily in one direction underneath.

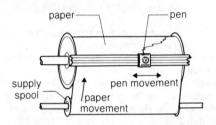

paper — — pen

supply
spool

pen movement

paper
movement

Checksum Digit A method of validating **data** entry. It is important to check that data is sensible as mistakes can often be made by the original data collector at the preparation stage or could be badly transmitted. Coded numbers can be summed and then divided by a particular number called the *modulus*. The answer should *not* contain a remainder. If it does, the coded number is not valid as a mistake has been made in it.

Example: to check the number 462347

        sum all the digits: 4+6+2+3+4+7=28

        divide by modulus (say odd number 7):

28 $\div$mod 7=0 (no remainder).
The coded number is therefore valid.

By using the checksum digit method, the possibility of a wrong number getting through a check is greatly reduced. See also **Weighted Check Digit**.

Chip The common name for an **integrated circuit**. It is a **solid state** circuit in which all the components are formed upon a single piece of **semiconductor** material. The first chip consisted of a transistor and a resistor and was created in 1959. Since then the number of components on a chip has nearly doubled each year. LSI (**large-scale integration**) means an integrated circuit with more than 100 **logic gates** or over 1000 memory **bits**.

CIM Acronym for Computer Integrated Manufacture.

CISC (Complex Instructions Set Computer) A term used to describe computer development which until now has been based on designing even more complex microprocessors so that eventually one **machine code** instruction is the result of translating one **high-level language** instruction. This means that microprocessors are designed to use thousands of machine code instructions no matter how little used they might be. In contrast, new **RISC** microprocessors with simpler designs have higher speeds and can emulate and run existing software much faster.

Clock An electronic device that provides pulses at fixed time intervals. These pulses can be used to control the operations of a computer so that they are all in step (**synchronous**). Clock pulses are generated by an **astable** multivibrator.

CM Abbreviation for Central Memory.

CML (Computer-Managed Learning) See **Computer-Assisted Learning**.

CMOS Acronym for Complementary Metal Oxide **Semiconductor**.

Coaxial Cable A cable containing two or more conducting wires, each insulated and surrounding the one before. For example, TV aerial cable; cables connecting a network of computers in, say, a school.

COBOL (acronym for COmmon Business Oriented Language) A worldwide **high-level language**

developed in America in 1959 for general commercial programming.

Code   A term used to describe a set of programming instructions for a computer, though it may also refer to the binary patterns used to represent **characters**.

Coded Number   The record number of an object. This can be made up, or coded, in a particular way to conform to a company or organization's particular computer system. Coded numbers can then be checked for validity by **checksum** or **weighted check digit** methods.

COM   Acronym for Computer Output on Microfilm, a process for converting computer output direct to microfiche or film, especially 35mm or 16mm film.

COMAL   A **high-level language** descended both from BASIC and Pascal.

Compact Disc – Interactive (CD-I)   A compact disc (an **optical disc** of approximately 5-inch diameter) which allows both read and write access, thus making it interactive with the user.

New programs and data are 'burnt' onto the disc surface as dips by a strong laser. A weaker laser is passed over the surface and the reflected distortion from the dips forms the data.

At present it is difficult to erase the contents and return to a perfectly smooth disc surface. The *WORM* (Write Once Read Many Times) technique overcomes this by writing new or revised data onto unused parts of the disc and making any previous contents inaccessible, thus giving the appearance of resaving programs or data. Since compact discs have a 600 megabyte capacity, it can be a long time before a disc is used up and a new one required.

Compact Disc — Read Only Memory (CD-ROM) An **optical disc** of approximately 5-inch diameter, on which data is digitally recorded as a set of dips in the surface. The reflected distortion from shining a weak laser beam across the dips forms the data which can be used for 'playback'. CD-ROMs are widely used in optical disc music players and can incorporate programmed search and memory facilities.

Optical discs for music are regarded as giving perfect playback, no matter how many times they are used (no hiss and crackles, as with a conventional vinyl record). As the disc is rigid and no parts touch the surface, tracks can be densely packed together. Optical discs have a 600 megabyte capacity and are well suited for computer applications needing vast storage. For example, the whole of Europe's telephone directories could be stored on a couple of discs, and in fact the Post Office stores all Britain's 24 million postal addresses on a 5-inch CD-ROM. The British Library is developing a complete catalogue of its books on a disc.

Compiler A language-translation program which converts instructions written in a **high-level language** into **machine code**. A compiler is different from an **interpreter** in that instructions (the source program) are entirely converted into machine code before being run and saved (object program). A compiled program requires more memory space but is faster to run and is excellent for already developed and completed programs.

Complement A method of subtraction on binary numbers. Subtraction is the opposite of addition. Complements methods use this principle. For example, to subtract 4 from 10:

Normal method: 10−4=6

Complement's method: What number added to 4 gives the answer? 4+?=10

One's complement involves adding to each binary digit to make 1 in the answer. In effect, all the digits are reversed. This is sometimes called *negation*.

Two's complement is sometimes called negation +1. The method is used to find the result of a subtraction. It also helps explain how binary numbers are expressed inside the computer's memory.

Complex Instructions Set Computer See **CISC**.

Computer An electronic data-processing machine that has three components

where the input and output may be **digital** or **analogue** and the process would involve storage, control and arithmetical operations. A computer differs from most other machines because it is versatile and not restricted to doing one particular job. A micro-computer has a **microprocessor** as its **central processing unit**.

Computer-aided Design   See **CAD**.

Computer-Assisted Learning (CAL)
Computer-Based Training (CBT)
Computer-Managed Learning (CML)
These three entries refer to the use of the computer in
education, the middle word in each case defining
the use. Note the other variations listed in the book
and in the abbreviations section at the end. In the case
of CAL the computer could display various pieces of
information and ask particular questions depending
on responses given by the user, thus assisting with the
understanding of a topic. CBT uses the computer as a
medium for the training course whereas with CML the
computer not only provides the course but directs the
student from one section to another according to
progress and records the standards attained.

Computer Bureau   A company which sells time on
its computer to many users. Thus a small firm can have
the use of a large expensive computer quite cheaply,
and in addition have the help of the bureau if needed.

Configuration   This word refers to the pieces of
hardware that make up the computer system.

For example, a common micro configuration might consist of a microcomputer with 512 Kilobytes (1/2 megabyte) **random access memory**, a 3.5-inch microfloppy disk with 720 Kilobytes capacity, a colour monitor and a dot matrix or laser printer.

(a) monitor

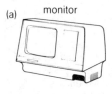

(b) microcomputer

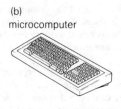

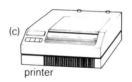

(c) printer

(d) disk unit

Console This is what the computer operator uses and may be a **visual display unit** plus a typewriter keyboard. This is called a *dumb terminal* because it does not have any processing power of its own.

Continuous Stationery Paper, which may be pre-printed forms, consisting of hundreds of perforated sheets which can be automatically fed through a **tractor-feed** printer by the **sprocket holes** along the sides.

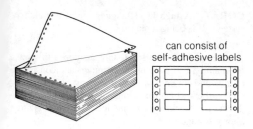

can consist of
self-adhesive labels

Control Character A **character** which when transmitted starts or controls a device.

For example: a computer output having a particular character at the beginning may be routed to a printer, whereas with a different control character at the front it might be displayed on a **visual display unit**.

Control Register A **register** whose function is to hold the address of either the current **instruction** or the next instruction that the computer has to carry out. Also called the *program counter*.

Control Unit This is the part of the **central processing unit** which makes the computer carry out, in turn, each **instruction** of a program.

45

CORAL A **high-level language** used in military systems. It is being replaced by **ADA**.

Core Store Before **solid state** memories this was the main type of store in all computers and consisted of rows and columns of small iron rings. They are like tiny washers which can be magnetized in one of two directions, clockwise or anticlockwise, thus giving **binary** storage.

Counter A name given to any device which continues to record 'the number of times' something is done. It might record the number of computer cards that are punched or, in the case of a program, the number of times a certain **loop** is carried out, though in the latter case the counter would be no more than a particular memory **location** whose value is increased by one each time.

For example: in a program when the computer expects, say, a 6-digit number, a counter could be used so that it waits for 6 digits but will accept no more.

Courseware These are the accompanying instructions that have to be followed together with the learning or training package run on the computer. Courseware may be printed so that it can be studied in the usual way but may be a part of the computer **software**.

CP/M Acronym for Control Program for Microcomputer, a widely used operating system which enables a range of software to be run on microcomputers.

CPS Abbreviation for Characters Per Second, a measure of the speed of a **printer**.

CPU See **Central Processing Unit**.

Cray Seymour Cray, the American designer of many of the most powerful computers in the world, which are named after him.

Critical Path This is a method of breaking down a large project into a series of ordered sequences. Each stage is then dependent on those before and predictions about time scales can be made. Though not necessarily associated with computers, the method of critical path analysis usually involves a large amount of calculation best done by a computer.

Cross Compiler A **compiler** used by one computer to produce a **machine code** program suitable for another, usually smaller, computer.

Cursor Generally a rectangle the size of a capital letter which appears (sometimes flashing) on the screen of a **VDU** to indicate the current display position. Pressing a key should result in that **character** appearing on the screen in place of the cursor which is then displaced one character to the right.

Cybernetics The study of computer control in comparison with the human nervous system.

Daisywheel Printer This **printer**, as its name suggests, has a wheel with arms like the petals on a daisy. At the end of each arm there are two letters and these are pressed forward by a hammer to print on paper using a typewriter ribbon. It prints at a speed of about 50 characters per second and is generally noisy.

10
characters
per inch

12
characters
per inch

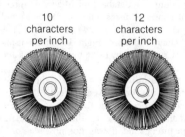

Data A general term for numbers, digits, characters and symbols which are accepted, stored and processed by a computer. Only when such data becomes meaningful to a person can we say we have **'information'**. Thus terms such as 'information processing' and **'information retrieval'** are really **'data processing'** and 'data retrieval'.

Database Really just files of structured **data** stored in a computer but arranged so that they can be accessed in many different ways for use in various applications. The idea is that the same data is stored only once but can be manipulated by the database management system so that data files can be shared by various pieces of software.

For example: a database might contain three files; one on names of firms, one on addresses and one on types of business. Access to all three files for a particular company might be made using the company's name or by using the company's address.

Data Communications This is the process of transmitting data between equipment, often over long distances. Particularly in the past, computers and equipment were made to different standards by manufacturers, and it was not possible for direct communication between them. Thus, intermediary *data packet* systems are used which can change data into a form which can be communicated forward and then on exit change the data into a form which can be used by the receiving computer.

For example, British Telecom run a Packet Switch Stream (PSS) system called *Broadband*. On entry the data is assembled so it can use the system and is moved forward in packets. At the required exit it is disassembled for use by the receiving computers.

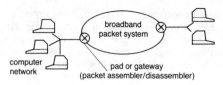

computer
network
pad or gateway
(packet assembler/disassembler)

The Broadband system can forward voice, data, image and fax traffic.

The international telecommunications committee (CCITT) has recently approved a new communications standard which, if adopted, will make it possible for all computers and equipment to communicate over long-distance public systems. This is the X.400 standard. Existing CCITT standards include V.24 (RS232C ports).

Datalogging A term used to describe the automatic collecting of **data** by a machine for a computer, the data being stored for later analysis.

For example: a **microprocessor**-controlled central heating system would repeatedly record data from the heat sensors in the different rooms around the building. This data could be kept and used to control the heating.

Data Packet Systems See **Data Communications**.

51

Data Processing (DP) The operation of collecting, storing, processing and transmitting **data**. A computer could be described as a data processing machine though a data processing system could involve clerical work and additional **hardware**.

Data Protection Act An Act of Parliament which came into force in May 1986. All organizations, businesses and institutions which hold computerized personal information on people have to register that fact. Individuals now have the legal right to view files held on themselves. There are some exceptions, such as police and medical records. A record containing wrong information can be ordered to be changed.

Debugging A computer program may contain errors and these have to be found and corrected. As these errors are called **bugs**, correcting them is known as debugging. The three main types of error are logic errors (the program subtracts B from A instead of A from B); **syntax** errors (the instruction rules have not been properly used); and **run**-time or execution errors (such as drawing with the same foreground as background colour).

Decimal An integer in the range 0 to 9 used in **denary notation**. Note that when working in denary (base 10) one uses the digits 0 to 1-less-than 10, that is 9. Similarly when working in a different base, say 6, one uses the digits 0 to 1-less-than 6, that is 5. In binary (base 2) we just use 0 and 1.

Decision Box A diamond-shaped symbol used in a **flowchart** to indicate a choice in direction. The choice is usually dependent upon the value of a **variable**.

For example:

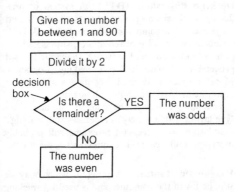

Decoder This is used to change **data** from one coded form into another. For example: an instruction in a program such as PRINT would be stored in **binary** and as such would have to be decoded by **logic circuits** before it could be carried out.

Denary Notation   Our normal number system where we count in tens using **decimals**. The digits 0 to 9 are used in the units column before we carry over to the tens column.

Desktop Publishing (DTP)   A system of producing professional-quality reports, booklets and magazines on a computer and peripherals. A DTP system usually consists of a computer, a **mouse**, a laser **printer** and associated software (integrated **word processing**, graphics and page-making programs). More complex systems also contain a scanner for reproducing black-and-white photographs.

Text and graphics can be made up into magazine-type layout with a variety of typefaces and headings. Standard word-processing programs will probably incorporate all these DTP features in a few years' time.

Diagnostic Routine   A program which may be supplied with the computer and is used for tracking errors in programs or for detecting faults within the machine. Useful for **debugging** programs.

Digit Any of the figures 0 to 9, though note that the number 747 has three digits but only two different **characters**. To a computer a digit is part of an item of **data**.

Digital Computer This type of computer only works with **data** represented in a digital form, usually **binary** 0's and 1's. It differs from the **analogue computer** in that it can store large amounts of data and can calculate very accurately.

Digitizer This is a device which converts analogue signals into **digits**; that is an **A to D converter** (analogue to digital).

For example: in order that a computer might record readings of temperature one would connect the recording device to a computer via a digitizer. As the temperature rises so there would be a continuously increasing voltage input to the digitizer which is repeatedly scanned by the computer. The computer records the increases in finite jumps, storing the **data** as **digits**. Although the jumps can be made very small (thus giving greater accuracy and more significant figures) they always exist in the computer data.

DIN Acronym for Deutsche Industrie-Norm, the German equivalent of **BSI**. Its industry standard for plugs, sockets and cables for interconnecting audio and video equipment has now been extended to cover computer terminals and peripherals.

Direct-Access Storage Unlike **serial access**, direct-access storage can be reached very quickly and without any reference to previously accessed locations. Sometimes called **random access memory** (RAM), the data or program can be accessed almost instantly without having to go in sequence from the beginning.

Disk (or **disc**) A flat circular plate covered in magnetic material which is able to store data on its concentric tracks. As the disk spins a read/write head travels from edge to middle selecting only the required tracks. Each track is divided into **sectors**. A format program is used to lay down the tracks and sectors on a blank disk. Disks allow fast **direct access** time compared to the much slower sequential access tapes.

Disk Unit A peripheral device consisting of a disk drive and one or more read/write units. Disks can be fixed in place (**hard disks**). Removable ones for microcomputers are called **floppy disks**. When inside the unit the disks are accessed by the read/write head as they revolve at high speed.

Documentation This usually accompanies a computer program and gives advice on how to use the package and what output can be expected. It may also include a **flowchart**, a program listing, a list of **variables** and testing procedures with sample **data**. Documentation is useful to the program user but is vital if modifications are to be made to the program.

Document Reader An input device for a computer whereby forms having marks in certain positions are read (can be at high speed) by a machine. For example, **magnetic ink** and **optical character recognition, marksense cards**.

DOS Acronym for Disk-**Operating System**.

Dot matrix printer A **printer** which forms characters on paper by printing a pattern of dots. The printing head consists of a set of horizontal needles mounted one above the other in a line. As the head moves sideways, certain wires are pushed forward to form a column of dots on the paper and several such columns form a **character**. Early matrix heads had seven needles but were unable to print lowercase descenders (the tail of a g or y). Now nine needles are used, but there are printers with 16, 18 and even 24 needles. A range of colours can be achieved by using, say, a four-colour ribbon and overprinting in different colour(s).

For example, a nine-wire dot matrix printer uses five dots for a small letter plus two above for capitals and two below for lowercase descenders:

An improved print is obtained by printing each character twice, particularly if the second print is slightly out of line with the first, making the gaps between the dots less obvious. This is often called 'near letter quality' (NLQ).

Modern dot matrix printers can print at up to 300 characters per second in draft mode and 60 characters per second in NLQ mode. They are preferred to **daisywheel printers** because they can print in a range of font styles and graphics and they are also quieter to operate. Although noisier and slower than **laser printers**, they have the advantage that because they are impact printers they can produce carbon copies of hard copy.

Double Buffering The use of two **buffers** in a computer where one can be analysed whilst the other is being filled and vice versa.

Double Word A facility of some microcomputers where two **words** can be operated as one double-length word. This enables a computer having 8-**bit** words to be used as a 16-bit word machine.

Downloading Used to describe the taking of **data** from a large machine (**mainframe**) to a smaller one (**microcomputer**). This process might use the telephone, the radio or the television to provide the link between the two.

Down Time The length of time during which a machine is not usable due to faults of some kind.

DP Abbreviation for **Data Processing**.

Dry Run This is the term for using pen and paper to work through a **program** by constructing a *trace table* (a table showing the program pathway of variables and important events such as decisions). By inputting data and following the pathway and events, run time or execution errors can be spotted. Dry running a program is an important part of developing programs and saves time and costs when it avoids the problem of having to recall sold programs from customers to correct bugs.

DTL Abbreviation for Diode Transistor Logic, a stage in the development of electronic **logic circuits**.

DTP Abbreviation for **Desktop Publishing.**

Drum A cylindrical device coated on the outside with magnetic material which is able to store **data**. One or more read/write heads move along the side of the spinning drum selecting the required track.

Dumb Terminal A **terminal** with no processing power of its own.

Dump A word used to describe the process of copying the **data** in a section of memory and sending it to a **peripheral** device (a printer, say) or to a **backing store**.

Duplex Operation A mode of transmission which allows **data** to travel in both directions at the same time. It also displays on the screen the **character** typed as well as sending it to the computer. *Half-duplex* allows travel in both directions but not at the same time.

Dynamic Stop When running a program it may be necessary to draw the operator's attention to some factor or other. A dynamic stop jumps the program into an infinite **loop** at the same time indicating an **error** condition. Only after interaction by the operator will the machine resume processing.

EAROM Acronym for Electronically Alterable **Read Only Memory**.

EBCDIC Acronym for Extended Binary-Coded Decimal-Interchange Code, a computer code for representing **alphanumeric** characters.

Echo This is used as a check when transmitting **data**. What is received is returned to the original point and compared with the original data. If they are the same then the transmission has been carried out correctly.

ECMA Abbreviation for European Computer Manufacturers Association.

Edge Connector Where the conducting paths on a **printed circuit board** are taken to the edge to form a connector. Most boards have several edge connectors allowing the board to be plugged into a socket.

EDI Abbreviation for **Electronic Data Interchange**.

Edit The task of changing and improving a program by adding or removing instructions or by modifying the **data**. Sometimes done with the help of a special program called an *editor*.

EFTPOS See **Electronic Funds Transfer at Point Of Sale**.

Eighty-Column Card The shape and size of **punched cards** vary according to the design of the computer on which they are used. However the most common are oblong in shape and have eighty columns, each column having twelve punched-hole positions.

Electronic Data Interchange (EDI) The system of exchanging invoices, orders and other forms by using phone lines, electronic mail and computers. Purchasers and suppliers have often to complete many documents before business can be concluded, and in international trade customs points between countries make business slow, frustrating and full of delays to complete. At present, a project involving some of the biggest international motor and chemical companies is testing such an EDI system. Standards of inter-change (**OSI**) have been agreed with the United Nations and the International Standards Organization (**ISO**). It is hoped that EDI will make the paperless transfer of documents into a reality. See also **Information Systems**.

Electronic Device A device whose operation depends mainly on the behaviour of tiny charged particles called electrons. If used to store **data** it would be known as an electronic **memory**.

Electronic Funds Transfer at Point Of Sale (EFTPOS) A system of direct communication between a bank's computer centre and retail outlets (shops, garages, service points). A point of sale terminal is used to feed data directly to and from a customer's bank account. In this way an account can be debited instantly for any products purchased.

The point of sale terminal often has a **light pen** attachment for reading **bar codes** (which communicates with automatic stock control/reordering systems) and a **magnetic strip** reader to provide data for the receiving computer. Prices and other transaction details could be obtained from **EPROM** chips within the terminal.

EFTPOS may herald the day of the cashless society, when we will rely on plastic cards and rarely use money.

Electronic Mail A system where **data** is sent from one place to another via a **telecommunications** link. A letter typed on a word processor could be changed or corrected and then sent via a satellite communications system from an office in one country to a **VDU** screen in another country. Here it could be held in **memory** until required and then answered in the same way: no paper, no stamp, no postman; just an 'electronic office'.

Electrostatic Printer This machine prints on paper by charging selected areas of the paper (similar to rubbing a balloon on your sleeve and allowing it to hold itself on to the ceiling) so that they can attract a fine dust which is then permanently fused to the paper by heat.

Emulator A piece of **hardware** (though can be software) which when attached to a computer makes it behave as if it was another type of computer. Thus programs prepared for one range of computers can, with the aid of an emulator, be run on another range of computers.

Encoder A device (such as a keyboard or position indicator on a turning shaft) which converts signals into the coded digital form required for the next process.

End Mark When working with a stream of **data** it is sometimes necessary to indicate the end of various items and this is done by using a particular code known as an end mark.

EPROM Acronym for Erasable Programmable Read Only Memory, a form of **read only memory** chip which can store programs or data. The data can only be erased by exposing the chip to strong ultraviolet light.

Erasable Storage A storage medium which can be used over and over again as new **data** overwrites the old data.

For example: magnetic tape or magnetic disk.

Erase The rubbing out of **data** that has been stored. However, unlike the rubbing out of a pencil line where nothing is left, in a computer it means replacing a code with another code that represents null data. It might be zeros but this is not necessarily the case. Each time data is stored, whether it is in the computer's memory or on disk or tape, this new data overwrites or erases what was originally stored.

Error This is said to have happened whenever the results that are expected do not appear. Errors in a computer system may be caused by software mistakes, faulty equipment or human operator mistakes:

1. There are three types of software error:
   (a) **syntax** errors: mistakes in using programming rules, e.g. PRIT for PRINT
   (b) logic errors: mistakes in the sequence of instructions, e.g.

   > If A = B THEN PRINT 'A and B same'
   > missing GOTO to jump over next instruction
   > PRINT 'A and B not equal'

   (c) **run** time/execution errors: these are found only when a program is run, e.g. words written in the same colour for foreground and background.

   Bugs in software can be found by using a **trace** program or **dry running** on paper (particularly in the case of syntax and logic errors.
2. Faulty equipment errors can be found by service engineers running special **diagnostic routines**.
3. Operator errors can be caused by a program being used at the wrong time or out of sequence. They also include accidental damage to or loss of the backing store.

Error Message When an error occurs it may be possible for the program to indicate what has gone wrong by putting a message on the screen. Such wording is known as an error message and helps the user find the fault quickly.

For example: 'cannot divide by zero at line 230' is

an error message which tells the operator that the
value of the denominator is zero at instruction number
230 in the program.

Exclusive-OR Gate   This is a **logic gate** which
operates with binary digits. Its output is of logic value
1 when any of its inputs have logic value 1 but not if all
the inputs are 1. (**Inclusive-OR** also outputs a 1 if all
the inputs are 1).

For example: with a two input exclusive-OR the
following **truth table** applies

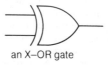

an X–OR gate

Input		Output
0	0	0
0	1	1
1	0	1
1	1	0

This gate could be used to sum two binary digits but
does not give the carry digit.

Execute A word used to describe the carrying out of a program or of just a single instruction.

Exit This would result from the last instruction in a **routine** which would send the computer back to the main program; or it could be the ending of the whole program.

Extended BASIC BASIC is a computer programming language. Extended Basic is any version which provides additional functions and facilities.

Facsimile   See **FAX**.

Fail-safe   This term is used to describe a computer system or **peripheral** device which is able correctly to stop itself working should a fault occur.

Fast Line   Rates of transmitting **data** are usually given in **baud**. **Prestel** transmits to the user at 1200 baud although data at this speed on telephone lines can get lost or muddled. Special direct lines, available from British Telecom, are able to transmit data at 48000 or 96000 baud. Such lines would be known as fast lines.

Fault Tolerant   Some computers are designed with backup circuits so that should there be a failure then its duplicate would automatically switch on. Sometimes a backup circuit 'mirrors' the activity of its main circuit so that no loss of data would occur during the switchover. Fault-tolerant computers are more expensive but deemed essential for applications where a computer failure would be almost disastrous, for example, in air traffic control.

FAX   Short form of the word *facsimile*, the scanning

of a document and converting the shading into electrical signals which can be transmitted via wires or radio waves. These signals are used to create a copy of the original document.

Feasibility Study This is carried out before a company buys a new computer system. A team of experts (system analysts) would study the problem to see whether a computer was necessary and what sort of machine would best suit the company.

Ferrite Core A ring-shaped piece of magnetic material the size of a pinhead or smaller. Just as a bar of iron can be magnetized N—S or S—N so a ring can be magnetized clockwise or anticlockwise, and this is used for storing binary 0's and 1's. Such cores are built in rows to form what is known as the **core store** of a computer.

FET Abbreviation for **Field-Effect Transistor**.

Fibre Optics The **modulation** and transmission of information on light along a glass or Perspex fibre. Light entering one end of a fibre is repeatedly reflected on the outside of the inner part until it reaches the other end. Total internal reflection takes place as two types of glass are used and this involves very little energy being lost at each reflection.

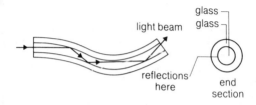

Such fibres are made very thin (less than 1 mm across) and are easily bent. Thus a cable consisting of many fibres can be laid in just the same way as normal copper ones. Up to 32,000 simultaneous telephone conversations can be carried for the same size of cable. Normal electrical signals (carrying data) are used to modulate a laser light beam which is sent to a receiver by an optical fibre.

Field-Effect Transistor (FET)   As opposed to the bipolar or **junction transistor** this **semiconductor** device works by regulating the current as it flows through a narrow channel. In terms of logic **gates** on a silicon chip the greater densities are achieved with FETs.

FIFO Acronym for First In, First Out, a type of memory system.

File Just as sheets of paper form a file in a filing cabinet so a computer file is a collection of structured data on a particular topic. The file can be in backing **store** or in the computer's **memory**. Each computer file has its own file name consisting of a limited set of **characters**, say six or eight.

File Inversion See **Inverted File, Sort**.

Firmware A word used to describe programs that are held in **read only memories** (ROM). These can be accessed very quickly and are not lost when the machine is switched off (non-**volatile** memory). Thus they do not have to be loaded into the computer as they are permanently available in the machine.

First Generation Computers These computers, built in the 1940s and early 50s, used electronic valves, whereas the **second generation**, built between the mid 50s and the mid 60s, used transistors. The **third generation** used integrated circuits.

Fixed Disk Store See **Hard Disk Store**.

Fixed-Point Arithmetic This system involves having the decimal point of every number in the correct place, though the position can be set before a calculation (i.e. all figures to two decimal places). This does limit the size of numbers though permits faster calculations by the computer. See also **Floating-Point Arithmetic**.

Flag An indicator added to the end of a piece of **data** which might be used to indicate an error or to make the **hardware** perform a branch to another part of the program.

Flat-Bed Plotter See **Plotter**.

Flip-Flop A basic electronic circuit which remains in one of two possible states until it receives a signal. It then switches over to the other state and waits for the next signal before switching back. Known technically as a **bistable** multivibrator it can be used as a storage device (two states, one for 0 and one for 1) or for division by two as two input pulses are required to get it to give out one pulse.

Floating-Point Arithmetic Unlike **fixed-point arithmetic**, these numbers are recorded as a set of digits together with the power to which their base is raised.

For example: the denary number 789.249 would be stored as (+0789249) and (+3). Most scientific calculators use this method which, although slower in calculations, gives a very much wider range of numbers. Note the convention of using E so that the number can be written as 0.789249E3 and that the EE key converts this to 7.89249E2.

Floppy Disk A flexible magnetic disk used for supplying and storing **data** for a **microcomputer**.

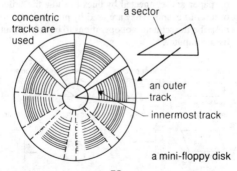

concentric tracks are used

a sector

an outer track

innermost track

a mini-floppy disk

When the disk rotates inside its cardboard jacket (say 300 r.p.m.) in a **disk unit** it becomes rigid and can be 'read' by the read/write head. The area used for recording is a band of concentric tracks each of which is divided into **sectors**. Disks may be single or double sided, double or quad density and soft or hard sectored. They are available in three sizes: 3.5-inch (microfloppy), 5.25-inch and 8-inch diameters. Developments in technology mean that the latest 3.5-inch microfloppies have up to 1.4 megabytes capacity, far more than those of other sizes.

Flowchart A set of special boxes or shapes drawn on paper and connected by lines to show the order of a set of events. They are used by programmers to describe the sequence of operations to be carried out by a computer.

terminator	action or process	decision	connector

input/output	annotation	lines crossing	lines joining

For example: using the symbols, this is the flow-chart for adjusting the pressure of a tyre:

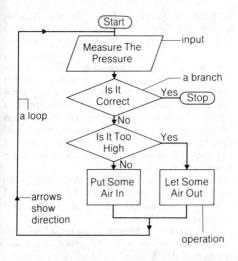

Format When used with **disks**, formatting refers to the laying down of tracks and sectors. This is often called initializing a new floppy disk.

In **word processing**, formatting means arranging

the layout of a piece of text in a particular way prior to its being printed.

FORTRAN (acronym for FORmula TRANslation) This **high-level language** was designed in the early 1950s as a scientific problem-solving language.

Fourth Generation Languages (4GLs) These are new types of programming **languages**, often called application and code generators because they cut development time and allow even non-experts to devise and code **programs**. Using predefined screens and English type commands, programmers and non-experts can define and design a computer system and any required programs. This is called making a template.

The main effort is in specifying detailed ideas and solutions, thus less time is actually spent coding and debugging. In fact, code generation can be almost automated after this stage.

4GLs also have prototyping features, allowing the eventual user to see how the finished system and programs will look. An added benefit is that potential problems can be spotted before coding takes place. This is why they are called high-productivity languages as they drastically cut development time. 4GLs are concise and easy to use and learn. Some specialize in particular applications. They call for computing personnel to have more knowledge of business/commercial situations rather than just straightforward computing skills. Some examples of 4GLs are Applications Factory, Powerhouse, Genesis, Sourcewriter. Some software packages now use 4GLs for complex tasks, like pagemaking in **Desktop Publishing**.

Frame An often misunderstood word in that it describes one screenful (about 150 words if all text) of information on the **Prestel** system. Prestel pages can consist of one or more frames. It is also used to describe one row of holes across a **paper tape** (which is the code for a single **character**) and one **bit** of store across a magnetic tape (a 0 or 1).

Function Code A computer instruction has two parts. The function, or **operation**, code states what has to be done (add, subtract, print) and the other part indicates on what (numbers, address).

Garbage The name given to meaningless **data**. Such rubbish is printed by a computer because of errors in the program or in the data or because the data belongs to another program. 'Garbage in—garbage out' (GIGO) is a well-known saying with regard to computers.

Gate Electronically this word refers to a part of the **field-effect transistor** though it is generally used to describe a **logic circuit** with several inputs and one or two outputs.

For example: an **AND gate** where the output depends on the logic state of the inputs. Such gates form the basic building units of all calculating chips.

Giga- The prefix meaning a thousand million, which in the US is called a billion. In computer technology it originally meant 1024 megabytes.

Gigabyte (GB or GByte) Originally the term for 1024 megabytes (MB or MByte) but increasingly being used to mean 1000 megabytes (1,000,000,000 bytes.)

GIGO Acronym for **Garbage** In, Garbage Out.

Grandfather With **data** that is **updated** on occasions it is normal to keep the last two versions as a safeguard. The three versions kept separately are known as 'grandfather', 'father' and 'son'.

Graphical Display Such a unit, rather like the screen of a television set, is used to display both text and drawings. Often a **light pen** or **mouse** can be used by the operator to get the computer to make changes to the display.

Graph Plotter See **Plotter**.

Half-Adder A **logic circuit** (which consists of a set of **gates**) which has two inputs and two outputs. It is used to add together two **binary digits** giving both the sum and the carry digit.

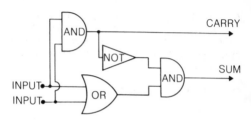

Half-Duplex See **Duplex Operation**.

Handpunch A mechanical device for punching holes. In the case of **punched cards**, on punching one (or two) of the twelve buttons the corresponding holes are punched and the card moves forward one column. In the case of **paper tape** the operator generally has a full keyboard, the tape moving forward after each character is punched.

Handshake This refers to signals such as 'ready to receive', 'transmit', 'interrupt', 'acknowledge', 'wait', which help to control data transfer between computers and peripherals.

Hard Copy   This is the printed output, usually on paper, which can be taken away and studied.

Hard Disk Store   A disk sealed into its unit. As the disk is not removable, the read/write head can sit extremely close to its surface and tracks can be densely packed together. Because of precision engineering, a hard disk has a far greater capacity than a floppy disk, typically up to 140 megabytes for micro equipment. As with floppies, data and programs can be added, revised and removed with software commands. Hard disks are also known as **Winchester disk drives**.

Hard-Sectored   This describes the way in which the length of a **sector** on a **floppy disk** is set. In this case small holes (say 6 or 12 in a ring) near the centre hole of the disk fix the length of each sector: as the disk revolves they indicate the change from one to the next.

Hardware   This is the name given to all the electronic equipment that makes up the computer system. If it can be picked up and carried then it is hardware as opposed to **software**.

Hardwired Logic This is the logic that is built in to an **integrated circuit** (or **chip**) by the manufacturer and refers to the wiring between **gates** as well as the gates themselves.

Hash Total Sometimes called a *batch total*, this is when the computer adds together a reference digit or number from each item in a file, thus giving a meaningless total or hash total. This is used on future occasions to check that all the items have been entered correctly.

Hertz The standard unit of frequency, named after the German physicist Heinrich Rudolph Hertz (1857-94), the first person to produce electromagnetic waves artificially. The basic unit (Hz) is one cycle per second so in the fast speeds of computing kilohertz (KHz), that is 1,000 hertz, and megahertz (MHz), one million hertz, are used.

Heuristic Program A program so written that each time it solves a problem it learns from itself and makes changes to improve its performance the next time.

Hexadecimal Notation (HEX) In this system one

counts in sixteens instead of tens. Usually the **digits** 0 to 9 are used and the letters A, B, C, D, E and F represent ten, eleven, twelve, thirteen, fourteen and fifteen. Whereas in a four-digit number in **denary** each digit in turn represents thousands, hundreds, tens and units, in HEX each digit would represent 4096's, 256's, 16's and units.

Thus:

$$A60B = (10 \times 4096) + (6 \times 256) + (0 \times 16) + (11 \times 1)$$
$$= 42507 \text{ in denary}$$

The reason for HEX being used by computers is because of the way numbers are stored. To store the numbers 0 to 9 in **binary**, four digits are required, 0000 to 0101. Thus for our normal numbers we have to use four binary digits, but with four binary digits we can store not just 0 to 9, but 0 to 15. That is 0000 to 1111. So by working in sixteens we can use all the available storage codes that the computer can offer.

High-Level Language A programming language in which each instruction is converted to several **machine code** instructions. A program can be entirely translated before running, using a **compiler**, or converted and run one instruction at a time, using an **interpreter**. High-level languages are problem-solving languages and can be used across many different computers. They are easy to understand as commands are near to English and very useful for developing programs, learning and education. Logo, Pascal, COBOL, C and BASIC are examples.

High-Resolution Graphics Most **microcomputers** offer some form of graphics whereby the programmer is able to plot points and draw lines. The graphics screen is divided into an 'X' horizontal axis and a 'Y' vertical axis. The whole area is composed of **pixels** (picture elements). As a rough guide, 640 by 250 pixels is considered high resolution, whereas 320 by 250 would be low resolution.

Special graphics **dumps** are required to read the screen and send the pixel data to a printer or plotter.

Hollerith Herman Hollerith (1860-1929) was an American inventor who realized that the results of the 1890 United States census could not be worked out by hand before the 1900 census was due and so devised a card-reading machine to analyse the census details.

The punched card code he invented allowed all twenty-six letters and the numbers 0 to 9 to be coded in twelve punching positions. Known as the Hollerith Code, it is still in use today.

Hopper   A device that holds punched cards ready for feeding to a **card punch** or **card reader**.

Housekeeping   These are **routines**, sometimes within a program, that are carried out when time is not of importance.
   For example: the setting-up of suitable fields or entry conditions or the allocation of areas of store or the updating of the master record-keeping file.

Hybrid Computer   This is a computer in which analogue and digital devices are interconnected so that **data** can be transferred between them. Usually found in science laboratories or as the controlling device in an industrial process.

Hz   The symbol for **hertz**.

IAR Abbreviation for **Instruction Address Register**.

IAS Abbreviation for **Immediate Access Store**.

IBM Abbreviation for International Business Machines Inc., The American multinational company which is the largest computer manufacturer in the world.

IC Abbreviation for **Integrated Circuit**.

ICL Abbreviation for International Computers Ltd, a British company which manufactures computers and distributes microcomputers.

Icon A pictorial symbol on the screen for a computer function, e.g. load, save. It can be activated by the cursor or a **mouse**.

Identifier A name or set of **characters** chosen by the programmer which indicates which **file** or which **variable** is to be used to hold data from the user at a particular point.

IEE Abbreviation for the Institution of Electrical Engineers, the British professional body.

IEEE A standard for **interfaces** set up by the American Institute of Electrical and Electronic Engineers.

IFIP Abbreviation for the International Federation for Information Processing.

Immediate Access Store This is used to describe those **memories** where **data** can be accessed in times of one millionth of a second (a microsecond) or less. Included would be those stores within the **central processor** and those directly addressable by the programmer.

Impact printer See **Printer**.

Inclusive-OR Gate This is a **logic gate** which operates with **binary digits**. Its output is of logic value 1 when any of its inputs has a logic value 1, otherwise it is 10.

an OR gate

For example: with a two input inclusive-OR gate the following **truth table** applies:

89

Input		Output
0	0	0
0	1	1
1	0	1
1	1	1

Incremental Plotter See **Plotter**.

Indexed Sequential Access This is the storing and retrieving of **data** from a sequence of stores whose **addresses** have to be first found by the computer from an index file.

Indirect Addressing This is where the address in a program instruction refers to another location which contains the real contents for use by the computer. This method can be used to access locations outside the maximum value of the **word**. For example, in an eight-bit word the computer can only directly access 127 locations.

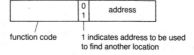

function code 1 indicates address to be used to find another location

Indirect addressing contrasts with the **address modification** method.

Information What is obtained from **data** by humans when they apply a set of rules.

For example: the data on this page is conveying information to the reader (the author hopes) because a set of rules (i.e. English words and sentences) are being applied by the reader. Note that a computer really only deals with data.

Information Retrieval A part of computing technology that allows speedy access to a structured file of data. In the past, finding out took time, allowing the user to think and plan. With today's on-line information retrieval, one has to plan the search route before starting as pages of information appear so quickly.

Information Systems A large **data communications** system consisting of a self-contained computer network connected to other computer networks either locally, remotely or between different countries. Its big advantage is the ability to move data speedily between different sites using **fibre optics** and/or microwave links. This can be used to integrate computer-aided design (CAD) and computer-aided manufacture (CAM) between office and factory.

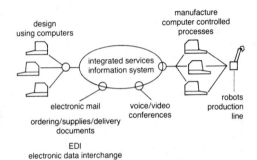

Examples: In Japanese car companies, a customer can choose a car seat from over 200 designs. Details are entered in the computer and passed to the factory site where computers control the manufacturing processes/robots. It is possible for the whole process, from design to delivery, to be completed in two hours.

Such computer-integrated systems may eventually lead to completely customized products at mass production costs.

A broadband information system will allow voice, video, data, images (fax) and electronic mail. Most countries are working towards a totally **integrated services digital network** (ISDN) phone system. Such systems will eventually herald what is called the 'information society'.

Information Technology (IT) The technology of the production, storage and communication of information, using computers and microelectronics.

Initialize The setting-up of the values of the **variables** at the start of a program so as to clear the values set by the previous run.

For example: **counters** would be set to zero or their initial values.

Ink-Jet Printer A non-impact **printer** which uses a fine jet of quick-drying ink. This is fired at the paper and forms characters as it lands. The ink droplets become charged as they are fired through the jet and can then be bent into shape by a varying electric field. Speeds as high as 200 characters per second can be achieved and the device has the advantage of not being limited by the number of metal characters that can be positioned for printing. In addition, character sets and type styles can be controlled by the program and many different languages can be printed with the same printer. With the addition of extra ink nozzles, extra colours can be printed.

Input Device   This is the device which is between the human being and the machine and enables both program and **data** to enter the computer.

For example: **punched cards** or **punched tape**. Also **light pen, keyboard, bar code** reader and **optical** or **mark sense** reader.

Input/output (I/O)   The data or information that is passed into or out of a computer.

Instruction   This is part of a computer program and it is the part that tells the computer what it should be doing at that stage.

For example: PRINT or ADD.

Instruction Address Register (IAR)   This **register** stores in turn the **addresses** of the instructions that the computer has to carry out. If during a program you could look inside this register you would find that it contained the address of the next instruction to be carried out.

Insulator   A material that has a very high resistance to electric current so that the current flow through it is negligible. One of the best insulators known is silicon dioxide which is created on the surface of silicon by heating.

Integrated Circuit (IC) or **Chip**   A **solid state** circuit in which all the components are formed upon a single piece of **semiconductor** material. LSI (**large-scale integration**) means an integrated circuit with more than 100 **logic gates** or over 1000 memory **bits**.

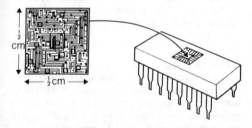

$\frac{1}{2}$ cm

← $\frac{1}{2}$ cm →

Integrated   Services   Digital   Network (ISDN)   An information system based on digital signals which will allow transmission of data, voice, video, imaging (fax) and electronic mail over the same wires. For all services to be offered **fibre optics** and microwave links will be used giving broadband wavelengths. Traditional copper wires have much narrower wavelengths. See also **Data Communications**.

Intelligent Terminal A **terminal** which has its own processing power and allows processing of data to be carried out without further access to the computer.

Intelsat Series of communications satellites operated by the International Telecommunications Satellite Consortium, from whose name the term comes.

Interactive Video (IV) A system consisting of computer, **optical disc**, video and monitor. The teacher/trainer can make course material made up of text, graphics, digitized pictures which are stored on optical disc. The video recorder can be interposed to provide film sequences as and when required.

The advantage for the student is a tailored individualized course. The computer uses the responses from the student as feedback to decide which particular learning path is most suitable.

IV is widely predicted to influence education. At present the system is being tested in trial schools and colleges. There is expected to be a vast market for computer-managed learning in industry and commerce.

Interface This is the circuitry (or **hardware**) needed between two devices so that they can be connected together. Such a circuit board might compensate for differences in speed-of-working or transmission speeds or might translate the codes. Often it is the type of transmission that has to be changed and the interface is attached inside one of the devices. Communication between such devices is called handshaking.

Interpreter A type of program which checks, translates and carries out a written program, one statement at a time. Most **microcomputers** are supplied with a **BASIC** interpreter which, though satisfactory for most purposes, is much slower running than a BASIC **compiler**.

Interrupt A system whereby a **peripheral** device

can stop the computer in its current task and use it to transfer **data** to or from that peripheral. The computer would then return to continue its work.

Inverted File A method of organizing a file so that groups are identified by 'keys'. Thus retrieving various groups is much quicker than by the normal method of searching every record. As **information retrieval** becomes widely used so *file inversion* becomes more important. See also **Sort**.

Inverter See **NOT Gate**.

I/O Abbreviation for **Input/output**.

IP Abbreviation for Information Provider, that is, the source from which the computer has gained information.

ISBN Abbreviation for International Standard Book Number.

ISDN See **Integrated Services Digital Network**.

ISO Abbreviation for the International Standards Organization, founded in 1947, which from its headquarters in Switzerland oversees the standardization of units of measurement and industry standards and of technical terminology, including computer terms.

IT Abbreviation for **Information Technology**.

Iteration This is a mathematical process by which one obtains an answer and then uses that answer to obtain a more accurate one. The new answer is then used to obtain an even better one and so on.

IV Abbreviation for **Interactive Video**.

Jacquard Joseph Jacquard (1752-1834) was a French inventor who developed the technique of using punched cards to store machine operating instructions. His automatic weaving loom was controlled by the punched holes in cards.

Job The term for the collection of activities involved in producing a piece of work on a computer. A job usually has many processes and can require several programs and program runs.

Job Control Language (JCL) A set of operating system commands designed for a particular computer, which is used to run a program. Such commands may involve loading a **compiler**, reading in the program, allocating memory and processing time and limiting the printer output. The same set of commands may be used regularly and in such case would be stored as a *job control file*.

Josephson Memory A magnetic memory device which was to operate at up to a hundred times faster than today's best **chips**, with even greater reductions in power consumption. The memory cells would be kept at very low temperatures using liquid helium. Because of major research problems encountered in the 1980s, development of Josephson memories has been stopped.

Joystick This is an input device for a micro-computer. The stick as it moves (usually in one of eight directions) is able to control the movement of a shape on the screen. It does this by working two potentiometers (like the volume control on a radio), one recording its movement in the X-direction and the other in the Y-direction. Often there are two joysticks enabling a screen game to be played by two players.

A similar device, the **mouse**, is used with business programs and **WIMP** environments.

Junction Transistor This is sometimes called the bipolar transistor or just 'transistor'.

As opposed to the **field-effect transistor** (FET) this

semiconductor device works by regulating the current across a junction or boundary between **p-type** and **n-type** materials. Their advantage over FET's is that they are faster acting.

Justify   This is the adjustment of the positions of words so that the left-hand or right-hand margins or both, are regular. This is easily done on **text** by a computer program before the words are printed.

For example: the paragraph above is both left- and right-hand justified whilst this paragraph is only left-hand justified, the lines being different lengths. **Word-processing** and text-editing programs have this justify feature.

K The symbol for **kilo** in computer storage, that is 1024. Note that the lowercase 'k' denotes 1000, as in kilogram, kilometre, etc.

Keyboard This is a device for coding **characters** on to **punched cards, punched tape** or directly into a computer. In addition to the standard typewriter (QWERTY) pattern there are numeric keys, user definable keys, **hexadecimal** keys and others.

For example: the **microwriter** keys.

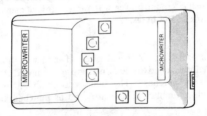

Key-to-Disk Unit A stand-alone device that allows **data** from a **keyboard** to be put directly on to **disk**.

Keyword Often used in **information retrieval** systems whereby items containing the given keyword are accessed by the computer and retrieved. In simpler systems only the titles of the stored items may be searched for the particular keyword though with some **mainframe** computers every word in the **database** can be checked.

Kilo-(K) This prefix generally signifies 'one thousand' as for example in a rate of transmission of **data**. 96 kilo**baud** means 96000 **bits** per second. However in terms of computer storage 1K is 1024 (which is 2 to the power of 10) and so 16K of memory means 16384 **bytes**.

Kimball Tag A small piece of card with holes, usually attached to goods in a shop and removed at the time of purchase. The holes encode the item or product number. These are used as **punched card**

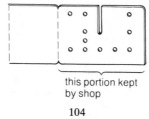

this portion kept
by shop

input for a computer, which is thereby able to keep sales records and provide management reports. Some shops have extra tags for sales, items returned, and exchange. Instead of holes, the data is sometimes coded in a magnetic strip on the tag.

Language   In order to tell a computer what to do we have to use a language it understands. In addition the language we use must be precise, with no chance of a double meaning. Such languages have been developed over the years from **machine code** and mnemonics to **high-level languages** like **BASIC** and **Pascal**.

Language Symbolique d'Enseignement (LSE)   A **high-level language** developed in the early 1970s in France for use in education.

Large-Scale Integration (LSI)   This is a measure of the number of **logic gates** on a single **chip**, about half a centimetre square. Small-scale integration (SSI) of about 1961 has less than 20; medium-scale integration (MSI) of about 1965 has between 20 and 100; and large-scale integration, developed about 1969, has between 100 and 5000. Today we have VLSI (above 5000), although the acronym LSI is the one that is commonly used. Note that the **microprocessor** is a special LSI chip but that the LSI chips used in watches and calculators are unlikely to be microprocessors.

Current practice is to produce an **uncommited logic**

array (ULA) chip which can have its logic gates connected in different ways for different customers. This is a cheaper and quicker way of obtaining a special type of chip as only one stage of manufacture is particular to that customer. However the design is limited by the original logic gates and the possible connections between them.

Lasercard Invented in California, this is a new form of plastic card, the same size as a bank or credit card, with a silver surface on the back. Up to 2 megabytes of data can be 'burnt' as dips in the surface. The lasercard can then be read by a weak laser. Data such as bank account details, medical history, digitized pictures, fingerprints, signatures or X-rays can be stored on it. Voice patterns and up to 800 pages of text can be stored on one card.

Updating is possible in a similar manner to **Compact Disc – Interactive** (WORM technique). A strong laser is used to burn new data onto unused parts of the card, with the added benefit of leaving an *audit trail* as an extra protection against misuse.

Given the vast range of data it can store, its security benefits and cheapness of manufacture, the lasercard is expected to be widely used across many applications in the 1990s, much as the common credit card is today. Research is at present being conducted into lasercards with 10 megabytes capacity.

Laser Printer This non-impact **printer**, which prints a page at a time, uses a dry copying process. The image is projected on to a light sensitive plate using a laser beam and the plate is covered with powder which is then transferred to paper. Such printers are capable of high speeds (20 pages per minute), good graphics (high resolution), and offer good colour but are expensive. Sometimes referred to as a *xerographic laser printer.*

LCD Abbreviation for **Liquid-Crystal Display**.

Least Significant Character In a set or row of characters the one in the furthest right-hand position is the least significant one.

LED Abbreviation for **Light-Emitting Diode**.

Left Justification This as opposed to **right justification** is the arranging of lines of text so that the left-hand edges are all in line. However it can also refer to **data** stored in consecutive locations all of which have been filled from the left though they may have a different number of spaces on the right.

Leibniz Gottfried Leibniz (1646-1716), a German philosopher and mathematician who, about 1670, designed a machine which could multiply and divide as well as add and subtract like **Pascal's** machine. This was the forerunner of the desktop mechanical calculating machine.

Library Software These are the programs and routines available to all the users of a particular computer. They form part of the facilities of the computer.

Light-Emitting Diode (LED) A small coloured device that emits light like a bulb. It is particularly useful as an indicator lamp in such things as computers, television sets and radios as it requires a very low current and works at low voltages. Used in the past in calculators and digital wristwatches but largely replaced by **liquid-crystal displays** (LCD) which require even less power.

Light Guide The name given to glass or Perspex fibre used to transfer optical signals. Light enters at one end and is totally internally reflected along the **fibre optic** — that is guided by the fibre.

Light Pen Sometimes called a *wand*, this is used

with a graphical display unit to allow the operator to draw, change and move sections of the picture simply by moving the pen across the screen. The pen is connected by cable to the computer and the operator uses keys to control the changes. A light pen can also be used to read **bar codes**. By running it across the light and dark shadings, the computer can read the signals and produce the bar code number.

Line Feed   This can be an instruction in a program or a button on a **printer**. In both cases we move to the next line down.

Line Printer   One type consists of a cylinder which has rows of characters. The A's are in one row, the B's in the next row, and so on. When a line is to be printed the cylinder turns so that all the A's are printed, then

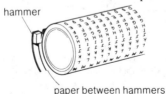

hammer

paper between hammers
and drum

turns so that all the B's are printed, then the C's; the whole line being printed in one revolution of the cylinder. Printing speed is between 500 and 3000 lines per minute but the lines printed are usually wavy.

For example: the line printer would print COLLINS COMPUTER GEM on one line by printing like this:

```
C          C
C          C       E    E
C          C       E    GE
C    I     C       E    GE
C    LLI   C       E    GE
C    LLI   C  M    E    GEM
C    LLIN  C  M    E    GEM
COLLIN     COM     E    GEM
COLLIN     COMP    E    GEM
COLLIN     COMP    ER   GEM
COLLINS    COMP    ER   GEM
COLLINS    COMP  TER    GEM
COLLINS    COMPUTER     GEM
```

Liquid-Crystal Display (LCD) Consists of a liquid whose molecules can be made to line up thus making it look darker when an electrical voltage is applied. Used in seven **segment displays** on watches and **calculators** as they require little power. Some liquid crystals change in colour with temperature and can be used as crude thermometers.

111

List Generally referred to as the listing on screen or paper of the program statements in number order. To follow the program statements in execution order one would use a **trace** facility.

Load The reading of program statements or **data** from **backing store** into the appropriate parts of the computing **memory**.

Location The name given to the places in a computer that are able to store **data**. Each location is identified and accessed by its **address** and the number of characters that can be stored in a location depends upon the particular machine.

Logic Circuit The basic building blocks of digital electronics often referred to as *logic gates*. **AND, OR, NAND** and **NOR** are all examples of logic circuits and it is these that make up the circuits on a silicon chip. In an **uncommitted logic array** (ULA) chip sets of logic circuits await interconnection to achieve the required circuit pattern.

Log In/On/Off/Out Is the term used when entering or leaving a large computer system from a

terminal. In this way the number of users can be limited and the type of use restricted.

Logo   A powerful **high-level language** invented by Simon Papert. Specially developed to teach structured programming and allow the exploration of ideas by both young and old. Its strengths include turtle graphics (building shapes and patterns by moving a screen marker), list processing, procedures and database management. Logo can also be used on control tasks with floor turtles and other microelectronic devices. It is widely used in education.

Look-Up Table   The dialling codes of all the towns and cities in the United Kingdom could be stored in a **table** in the **memory** of a computer. By typing in the place name, say Cambridge, the computer would use a look-up table to find the correct dialling code which would be 0223 in this case. Such a table would be arranged as an **array**.

Loop   Just as a loop of thread comes back to where it started so does a loop in a computer **program**. One difference is that the program continues to loop back until a certain condition is satisfied.

For example: the sorting of a set of numbers into

ascending order would involve the computer in carrying out a sequence of instructions over and over again (a loop) until all the numbers are sorted. One way is to:

COMPARE THE FIRST AND SECOND NUMBERS
IF FIRST IS GREATER, INTERCHANGE NUMBERS
NOW REPEAT THIS LOOP WITH SECOND AND THIRD NUMBERS

and so on. When all the numbers have been dealt with

REPEAT LOOP

starting with first and second numbers again. A run through of all the numbers without any changes means that they are in order. Note that a loop inside another loop is called a nested loop.

Low-Level Language The name given to a computer **language** which is similar to and easily converted into **machine code**. Each **instruction** is converted into one machine code instruction and is executed by the computer as a single operation. Such languages are difficult to program as they depend on the type of CPU used and are not portable across different computers. For example, popular low-level languages are 6502, Zilog X80 and Intel 80286 assembly. They are used when speed is of importance. With a high-level language (such as BASIC or FORTRAN) one instruction would involve many machine code operations but are easier to program.

LPM Abbreviation for Lines Per Minute, the speed at which printers produce hard copy.

LSI Abbreviation for **Large-Scale Integration**.

M The symbol for **mega-**.

Machine Code This is the coding that makes the computer carry out its various tasks. The types of instruction and the way they have to be written are specified by the computer manufacturer. Machine code programming has often to be done in **binary notation** and is used when fast operation is required.

For example: **instruction** number 634 might be to subtract (code 2) the contents of **location** 102 from the contents of 101 and put the answer in location 103. This might be machine coded as:

$$634\ 2\ 101\ 102\ 103$$

It should be clear that programming in machine code is slow and tedious. The programmer has to keep track of what is held in each location and specify these locations in each instruction. To make things easier manufacturers supply an assembly language or **assembler** which uses words and letters to represent operations and **addresses**.

$$SUB\ A,B,C$$

would mean subtract the value of B from the value of A and let C be the value of the answer. The assembler translates each instruction into one machine code instruction. For easier programming a **high-level language** such as **BASIC** is used and the instruction becomes:

$$LET\ C=A-B$$

A **compiler** or **interpreter** would then be used to translate such an instruction into machine code, though many machine code instructions would be required for each high-level language instruction.

Magnetic Ink This is used when printing characters on forms which can be automatically read or sorted by machine as well as by people. The characters are distinctive in that they are made up of thick and thin lines:

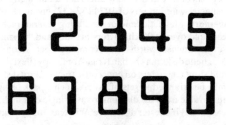

117

For example: the numbers along the bottom of each bank cheque are printed in magnetic ink. On receipt of a completed cheque the bank staff type the amount on to the cheque itself in magnetic ink and using a magnetic ink **character** reader linked to a computer all the necessary calculations and deductions are carried out automatically. Magnetic ink is used for applications which need high security and fairly indestructible printing.

Magnetic Memory   Just as a bar of iron can be magnetized with a north pole at one end and a south at the other (or the other way round) so other magnetic materials can be magnetized in two ways. This is used to represent a 0 or a 1 and is thus able to store **characters** in **binary notation**. Magnetic **core store** consists of tiny iron-type washers half a millimetre in diameter wired in sets of 1024 (32×32) giving 1K of **memory**. Magnetic **tape** or card using several tracks can hold over 1000 **characters** per inch and transmit several inches worth to a computer per second. Magnetic **disks** may be hard (rigid) or floppy (flexible) and store characters on concentric tracks. Hard disks may be arranged in sets of say six, such a pack being removable from the **disk unit** or as a single disk in the case of a **Winchester disk drive**. Whereas **floppy disks**

would hold a few hundred kilo**bytes**, hard disks hold several megabytes.

Magnetic Strip   A small band of magnetic material across the back of a plastic card, shop tag or intercity rail ticket. Data can be magnetically encoded as a series of binary digits. Limited storage of approximately 64 characters means only main essential details can be encoded, for example, sorting codes and account numbers on bank cards, or product numbers on shop tags.

Mainframe   This term is used to describe the **central processing unit** (CPU) of a large computer which has many **terminals**. Originally the words referred to the framework used to hold the CPU and **arithmetic logic unit** (ALU).

Main Store   This is the **memory** of the computer that can be accessed immediately. **Core store** and **solid state** memory are used for the main store whilst magnetic tape and disk are used as **backing store**. Also called **immediate access store**.

Maintenance Contract   Most computer manufacturers and computer repair companies offer service contracts on equipment. Such contracts may include

119

preventive maintenance whereby the machine is serviced regularly in addition to guaranteed call-out times (i.e. the engineer will visit four times each year and within 24 hours of a fault being reported). Some maintenance contracts include labour charges but not the cost of replacement parts: a full service contract would include both.

Mark-Sense Cards   Computer cards (which may be punched cards) divided into columns allowing spaces for marking with a pencil line. (Mark-sense forms are also available.) These marks can then be read electrically by a machine (mark-sense reader) linked to a computer or card punch. Similar to optical scanning where the marks are read by a light sensor. Both methods are useful for collecting and analysing responses to multiple-choice type questions.

Matrix Printer See **Dot Matrix Printer**.

Medium Scale Integration (MSI) See **Large-Scale Integration**.

Mega- The prefix which normally denotes a million, but which in computer terminology stands for two to the power 20, i.e. 1,048,576.

Megabyte (MB or Mbyte) In computer terminology usually 1,048,576 **bytes**, although the use of megabyte being taken to equal 1,000,000 bytes is increasing.

Memory A computer's memory is made up of its **main store** and its **backing store**. Sizes are measured in **bytes** and are given as so many K meaning **kilobytes**. (**Data** or program **instructions** may be stored.)
For example: a 512K RAM microcomputer.

Memory Mapping Items of **data** are often more easily accessed if they are stored in an **array**. However the computer **memory** consists of **locations** one after the other, and data, though arranged in an array can be stored sequentially. The arranging or mapping of arrays in this way (in a 'known' part of the memory) takes less space than arrays created in a **high-level language**. Memory mapping is also useful for sending data to **peripherals**, in particular to a visual display unit (VDU). Here data is made to appear on a peripheral device simply by putting it in a certain part of the **immediate access store**.

Memory-Switching System As its name implies this communications system uses a computer to accept messages from its terminals, stores them if necessary and then transmits them to other terminals as indicated by the message.

MICR Abbreviation for **Magnetic Ink** Character Recognition.

Microcomputer A computer which uses a **microprocessor** chip such as the Zilog Z80A, the Intel 80386 or the Motorola 68030 for its central processor.

Microelectronics That section of electronics which uses extremely small electronic parts. **Integrated circuits** are one example where cost, size, weight and power consumption have been reduced considerably, coupled with an increase in reliability.

Microfiche   The name given to a photographic-like slide (or film in the case of 'microfilm') which is viewed using a special type of projector. Pages of print, diagrams and graphs are considerably reduced in size and stored in this way. A 6×4 inch microfiche could hold up to 250 pages whereas a continuous roll of microfilm might hold 2000 pages. Computer **output** can be directly put on to microfiche or microfilm using a cathode-ray tube (CRT) picture (which is reduced in size) or a special laser printer. In addition to the size there is a considerable weight reduction compared with printed paper output. Using special machines it is possible for a computer to select and read pages from microfilm.

Microfloppy   At present the most popular form of magnetic disk for microcomputers. It consists of a 3.5-inch disk inside a hardened plastic case with a sliding cover which reveals the region accessed by the read/write heads of the microcomputer. It spins at

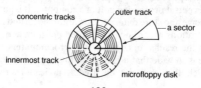

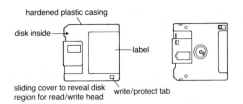

hardened plastic casing

disk inside

label

sliding cover to reveal disk region for read/write head

write/protect tab

a typical 3.5 inch microfloppy

around 300 revs per minute. Data is recorded along concentric circle tracks divided into sectors. There are approximately 135 tracks per side.

As the disk is rigid, data and tracks can be tightly packed together and the read/write heads can be very close to the surface. Consequently, microfloppies can have up to 1.4 megabytes capacity, far more than other floppies.

Microprocessor A special LSI **chip** that is used as the **central processing unit** of a computer. It is able to receive and store **data**, perform arithmetical and logic operations according to its stored program and give out the results. In addition to **microcomputers** their use is so wide that it is difficult to suggest an area in which they will not be used. Applications today include cookers and washing machines, cars and aircraft, machine tool control and remote monitoring of oil fields, video machines, bank cash dispensers and public telephone boxes.

Microwriter A portable gadget with a six-key **keyboard** (designed to replace the traditional **QWERTY** keyboard), a one-line display and a **memory**. By pressing different groups of keys different **characters** are put into the memory. Used to write, store and edit letters and reports anywhere (say on a plane or train) which can if required be transferred to a word processor on return to the office. Since the rise and popularity of portable computers its use has declined.

Minicomputer The minicomputer is the name given to small-sized machines that, in comparison to **mainframe** computers, have limited **memory** and a few **peripheral** devices. Being between the fixed-position mainframe and the portable **microcomputer** in size (similar to a wardrobe) it is generally used to do one specific job.

Minifloppy A form of **random access memory** for microcomputers. It consists of a 5.25-inch flexible

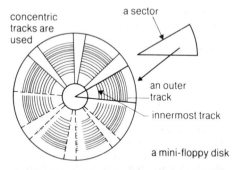

concentric tracks are used

a sector

an outer track

innermost track

a mini-floppy disk

magnetic disk inside a cardboard cover which has sections cut away for the disk drive unit (**disk unit**) and the read/write head to access the disk. When spinning at around 300 revs per minute the disk is rigid and the head moves in a straight line between the centre and the edge. Just as a cassette tape recorder uses parallel tracks on a tape so a disk drive uses concentric circular tracks on a disk. These circular tracks, around 40 in number each side, are divided into sectors and although the length of track in a sector is shorter near the middle of the disk it still takes the same time to pass the head. Thus data is more compact on the inner tracks of a disk. A minifloppy disk in its cardboard holder looks like this:

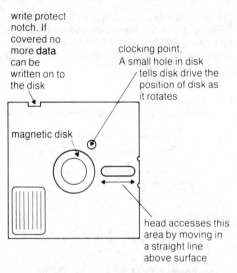

write protect notch. If covered no more **data** can be written on to the disk

clocking point. A small hole in disk tells disk drive the position of disk as it rotates

magnetic disk

head accesses this area by moving in a straight line above surface

As the **microfloppy** is rigid it is less vulnerable to damage than the minifloppy and is overtaking it in popularity.

MISP Abbreviation for Microelectronics Industry Support Programme.

Modem Acronym for MOdulator/DEModulator. This is a device for connecting two computers by a telephone line. It consists of a modulator that converts computer signals into audio signals and a corresponding demodulator.

Modulation The technique of using **data** signals to modify a transmitted wave so that the wave carries the

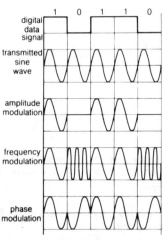

data signals. There are three ways in which a wave can be affected — by changing its amplitude (size) or its frequency or its phase. By varying one of these using a **modem** a data signal can be superimposed on a carrier wave.

Modulator/demodulator   See **Modem**.

Modulus   In an arithmetic system of remainders the integer that is used to divide another integer, the result of which is the remainder. For example, $11 \div \mod 7 =$ remainder 4. Moduli are used in **checksum** and **weighted check digit** operations.

Monitor   Most **microcomputers** will display their output on a television set, the signal being accepted via the aerial socket. For better definition, particularly with graphics, a monitor is required which accepts a **video** signal. This signal has a lower frequency though it can be either black and white or colour. In addition there are RGB monitors which accept separate signals for the three colours, red, green and blue, which make up the picture on a colour screen. The word monitor is also used to describe any device or a part of the operating system that examines what is happening in a computer system and takes action if something is wrong.

Most Significant Character The **character** on the extreme left of a set of characters.

Motherboard Some **microcomputers** consist of more than one **printed circuit board**. There may be a board to control access to the **disk** drives; one to provide **high-resolution graphics**; one for colour; one to support the input/output user ports; and so on. The board that holds and supports all the other boards is known as the motherboard.

Mouse A desktop device which has a tracker ball underneath. When moved about, it relays position and direction and so guides a pointer across the screen. It takes away the need for keyboard instructions as the pointer can be directed to an icon (a pictorial symbol) and functions can be selected by using the buttons on its top. The mouse is part of the **WIMP** environment and is also extensively used in CAD, word processing and graphics programs.

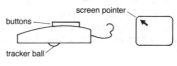

MPU   Abbreviation for **Microprocessor** Unit.

MS-DOS   A popular disk-operating system (DOS) produced by the Microsoft Corporation.

MSI   Abbreviation for Medium-Scale Integration. See **Large-Scale Integration**.

Multi-Access Processing System   Also called *time-sharing* system, this consists of a central computer with a specialized operating system. Many users on dumb terminals can be linked to the central computer which polls (checks) each incoming line in turn. If a terminal wants access to the CPU, data is transmitted from the **multiplexor** or attached backing store, down a fast input link to the CPU. The data is processed very quickly and returned. This is called roll in—roll out. Because of the speed with which each terminal line is polled and processed (**response time** is

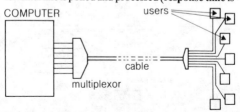

normally within five seconds), terminal users often think they have sole use of the computer.

Multi-access processing systems are used for single applications (often over large geographical areas) requiring central processing. For example, holiday/ airline booking; the police national computer; the Inland Revenue tax system; and ATMs (automatic teller machines or cash cards).

Multiplexor A device which controls the trans- mission of **data** between a computer and its many users. The multiplexor is able to switch very quickly so that data along a single wire can be routed from or to many different wires each one behaving as if it had continuous contact. Often multiplexors are used in pairs some distance apart each having many connections though only one path exists between them. This might be of wire, glass fibre or microwaves.

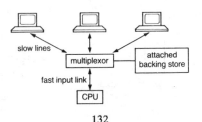

Multiprinter A lightweight electronic typewriter with its own 6000-byte memory and a liquid-crystal display. By using a special interface, it can be operated as a **dot matrix printer**.

Multi-Task Processing A specialized operating system which allows several programs to be held in the computer's memory at the same time. The operating system works out a processing priority so that peripherals such as printers are kept busy while the CPU can do any processing/calculations required. It gives the appearance of doing all its jobs together, but in fact little bits of each job are being done one at a time.

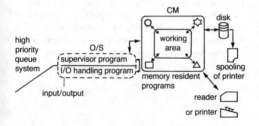

The big advantage of multi-tasking is that all equipment, especially expensive peripherals, is kept busy most of the time, thus giving value for money. Additionally, printer 'spooling' gives the CPU more freedom to get on with processing other data.

New types of multi-tasking software are now available, combining a specialized operating system with applications programs, for example Microsoft Windows, a **WIMP** set of programs.

Multivibrator   A basic electronic circuit that can be built using two transistors and a few components. There are three types:
(a) The **astable** multivibrator which continuously switches from one of its two states to the other and is used in computers as a clock.
(b) The **bistable** multivibrator which rests in one or other of its two states and is used to store a **binary digit**. Sometimes known as a **flip-flop**.
(c) The monostable multivibrator which when switched to the other state always reverts after a fixed time to the first state and is used for fixed timing or as a delay circuit.

NAND Gate   A logic gate the same as **NOT AND** (Not AND) whose **truth table** with two inputs would be:

Input		Output
0	0	1
0	1	1
1	0	1
1	1	0

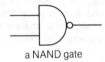

a NAND gate

It is worth noting that by joining the two inputs together on a NAND gate it becomes a **NOT** gate or an inverter.

Input	Output
0	1
1	0

135

Napier John Napier (1550-1617), Scottish mathematician who invented a very simple device for doing multiplication, known as Napier's Rods. It consisted of a set of eleven rods divided into numbered sections which when put side by side enabled multiplication by a single digit. Thus to multiply 634 by 58 the results of 'times 50' and 'times 8' were added together. He also pioneered the use of decimal notation but is best remembered as the person who invented logarithms, thus enabling complicated multiplication and division to be done easily. This invention led to slide rules and simple calculating machines, the forerunners of today's computers.

NCC Abbreviation for National Computing Centre.

Negation The operation of changing something into its opposite. The negation of the binary number 101 would produce 010. Each **binary digit** is changed to the opposite one. 'Negation plus one' enables one to find the **two's complement** of a binary number, the advantage being that we can use the normal rules of addition and subtraction with negative numbers.

For example:

Number	Negation (1's complement)	Negation + 1 (2's complement)
0101	1010	1011
010100	101011	101100
0111	1000	1001
0110 (+6)	1001	1010 (−6)

The third column is the 'two's complement' of the first column. In a system of positive and negative binary numbers the leftmost **bit** is used to indicate the sign; 0 for positive, 1 for negative. However with a 1, only the first bit is negative (place values are −8, +4, +2 and +1) thus the last line of the table above tells us that −6 (from −8+2) is the two's complement of +6 (+4+2).

NEQ Abbreviation for **Non-Equivalence Gate**.

Network This is where many computers are linked together to share printers, disk drives and other peripherals. Data can be transmitted at high speeds, and each user is able to access all the facilities.

Networks have specialized operating systems to control the flow of data, form queues for the use of peripherals and give passwords and security features to users. Networks are often called 'distributive processing systems'. A network of computers cabled together within a building or close area is called a 'local area network'. When users are remote from the central facilities and gain access via a **modem**, this is called a 'wide area network'.

NLQ Abbreviation for Near Letter Quality. See **Dot Matrix Printer**.

Noise Noise is the cause of errors in **data** that has been transmitted via a telephone wire. Random changes in voltage, frequency or phase can cause a change in the signal being transmitted and this results in the wrong code arriving at the receiving end. This problem is greatly overcome by using **digital** signals for transmission.

Non-Equivalence Gate (NEQ) This is a logic **gate** which operates with **binary digits** and is also known as the **exclusive-OR gate**. Its output is of logic value 0 only when all its inputs are the same. (Note that with an **inclusive-OR gate** the output is of logic value 1 when any of its inputs has a logic value 1).

a NEQ or X–OR gate

For example: with a two-input NEQ or X-OR gate the following **truth table** applies:

Input		Output
0	0	0
0	1	1
1	0	1
1	1	0

This gate could be used to find whether or not two binary digits are the same: it could also be used to sum two binary digits but it does not give the carry digit (that is, when adding 1+1 in **binary notation** we get 10 where the 1 is the carry digit and the 0 is the sum).

NOR Gate A logic **gate** the same as **NOT OR** (Not OR) which operates with **binary digits**. Its output is of logic value 1 only when all its inputs have a logic value 0 otherwise it is 1.

a NOR gate

139

For example: with a two input NOR gate the following **truth table** applies:

Input		Output
0	0	1
0	1	0
1	0	0
1	1	0

Normalize When working with **floating-point arithmetic** it is necessary to adjust each number so that it has the required number of digits after the point. The number is then said to be normalized.

NOT Gate This is a logic **gate** sometimes known as an *inverter*. The output is always the opposite of the input:

Input	Output
0	1
1	0

a NOT gate

When combined with an **AND** or an **OR gate** it inverts the output to give a **NAND** or a **NOR gate** respectively.

n-Type The way in which a **semiconductor** such as **silicon** conducts electricity can be changed greatly by adding a small amount of an impurity. Some impurities such as arsenic increase the number of electrons ('n' means more negative) and thus give n-type silicon. Transistors are made by combining n-type and **p-type** materials together.

Number Cruncher The name given to computers (usually **mainframe**) whose task is to carry out large mathematical calculations.

Numeric Referring to numbers. In **denary notation** this would use the digits 0 to 9. A numeric **keyboard** would have ten keys, one for each number.

7	8	9
4	5	6
1	2	3
0		

OA Abbreviation for Office Automation.

Object Code A program written in a **high-level language** is called a **source** program. A **compiler**, with or without an **assembler**, is used to produce a binary version of the source program in object code. This is in fact **machine code** which the computer understands and contains **data** as well as **instructions**.

OCR Abbreviation for **Optical Character Recognition** or Optical Character Reader.

Octal Notation In this system one counts in eights instead of tens, using the digits 0 to 7. Whereas the three positions in denary represent hundreds, tens and units, in octal they represent 64's, 8's and 1's. For example:

$$764 \text{ in octal} = (7 \times 64) + (6 \times 8) + (4 \times 1)$$
$$= 448 \quad + \quad 48 + 4$$
$$= 500 \text{ in denary}$$

To change from octal to **binary notation** each digit is converted in turn. 7 is 111, 6 is 110 and 4 is 100. So

$$764 \text{ in octal} = 111110100 \text{ in binary}$$

(Check $256 + 128 + 64 + 32 + 16 + 0 + 4 + 0 + 0 = 500$)

OEM Abbreviation for **Original Equipment Manufacturer**.

On/Off Line A term used to describe whether or not a terminal user is connected to the computer. Often terminals off line are used for **data** preparation though if they have their own processor they can operate as an independent computer.

Operand A **machine code** instruction can be divided into two parts. First, the operator (using an **operation code**) controls the process to be done (this might be print or load the **accumulator**). Second, the operand controls which memory **locations** are used and, for example, to which port or device the **data** is to be sent.

For example: a machine code instruction using a 24-bit **word** might be arranged in 8 and 16 bits.

★★★★★★★★	★★★★★★★★★★★★★★★★

OPERATOR   OPERAND
8 bits   16 bits
255 processes   65536 different **addresses**

Operating System A set of integrated programs which help control an entire computer system. It forms a background between the hardware and the user's (application) programs. Operating systems control peripherals, save and load programs, interface with the user, giving messages should things go wrong, provide security features (passwords, restricted access), and generally manage the operation of the disks. Large computer systems often have specialized operating systems which make the best of the expensive equipment provided. A **job control language** consisting of commands and instructions allows the user to communicate with these operating programs. Popular operating systems include CP/M, MS-DOS and OS/2.

Operation Code The part of a **machine code** instruction which says what has to be done has, itself, to be coded. The code used is called the operation code and although it is in **numeric** form it would mean such things as 'print', 'add' and 'subtract'.

For example: the operation code for 'print' might be 13 and so to print the contents of **location** 17 a programmer might code

| 13 | 0017 | or | 13 | 17 |

However in **binary notation** this would be

| 00001101 | 0000000000010001 |

Optical Character Recognition (OCR) A device which is able to recognize normal typed **characters** like A, B, 6, ? and provide corresponding input to a computer. At the present time such a machine would have difficulty in reading handwriting though certain types of print are easily read.

The following are OCR characters:

Example applications are the numbers at the end of a gas or electricity bill for recording payment, and the automatic sorting of typed postcodes by OCR machine.

Optical Disc Also called a video disc, this disc which is read by using a light (laser) beam is used for storing **data**. Changes in the way the light beam is reflected as the disc revolves are used to provide binary code for video playback on a music player, a television screen or a computer.

A **compact disc** is an optical disc of approximately 5-inch (30 cm) diameter. CD-ROM (read only

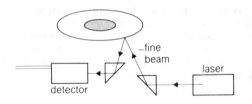

memory is the most popular form, used for music and video players as well as for storing vast amounts of fixed data. CD-I (interactive) is a new form for computer applications. Called WORM (write once read many times), it saves new data to unused parts of the disc. Compact discs have about 600 megabytes capacity.

Optical Mark Reader   This device does no more than detect the presence or absence of a pencil mark in certain places on sheets of paper or computer cards. It is sometimes guided as to the positions to be read by clock marks (thick black lines) printed down one edge. Examination Boards often use an optical mark reader to record candidates' answers to multichoice type questions.

Oracle   This is the name of the Independent

Broadcasting Authority's **teletext** service which transmits **data** along with the normal television programme transmissions. Each page is transmitted in turn in a never-ending sequence as a form of 'dots' tucked away out of sight at the top of the television screen. With a teletext decoder this data can be made to fill the screen (or be superimposed over the picture) one page at a time. Oracle includes advertising pages and provides local information by transmitting a selection of different pages in different regions. The data of page 175 onwards when loaded into particular **microcomputers** provides **software** for those machines. Software transmitted in this way is known as **telesoftware**.

OR Gate　This is a logic **gate** which operates with **binary digits**. Its output is of logic value 1 when any of its inputs have logic value 1.

an OR gate

For example: with a two input OR gate the following **truth table** applies:

Input		Output
0	0	0
0	1	1
1	0	1
1	1	1

This is the **inclusive-OR gate** as opposed to the **exclusive-OR** or **non-equivalence gate** which gives 0 if 'all' the inputs have logic value 1.

Original Equipment Manufacturer (OEM) A term used to describe the manufacturer who makes and sells a piece of equipment which may include products of other manufacturers. Thus these other manufacturers would point out that their products were suitable for use by an OEM.

For example: the original equipment manufacturer of a certain type of printer might use a print-head mechanism or an **integrated circuit** from another supplier.

OSI Abbreviation for Open Systems Inter-connection, a model devised by the International Standards Organization for **network** communication involving hardware and software applications.

OS2 A new **operating system** designed by IBM.

Output The name given to the available results of the computer's work. It may be sheets and sheets of paper on to which the results have been printed or it might take the form of a picture on a television or **monitor** screen. Other examples of an output device include a **graph plotter, card punch, paper tape** punch and **microfiche**.

Overflow When a computer carries out arithmetic, say adding two numbers together, it is possible for the answer to be too big for the computer to store in the space allowed. The term overflow is used to describe this situation though generally a computer signals the problem to the user when it happens. Overflow is much more likely to occur with **fixed-point arithmetic** than with **floating-point arithmetic**, the latter being able to store numbers up to 10^{38} using two eight-bit **words**, that is a number in **denary notation** with thirty-eight noughts.

Overlay A useful way of overcoming the problem of not having enough **main store** in a computer. The **program**, which is too long, is loaded and run in sections, more of the program being called into memory as and when required. Each new section overlays and rubs out a previous section. Overlays are commonly used with **word processing** programs.

Packet Switch Stream (PSS) See **Data Communications**.

Packing Density A measure of the amount of **data** that can be held by a **backing store** usually stated as so many **bytes** or so many **bits** per unit length.

For example: 800 bits per inch for half-inch magnetic tape.

Paddle A device shaped like a paddle for controlling the movement of an image, usually the cursor, on the screen. Used chiefly in games, it has been overtaken in popularity by the **joystick** and, more recently, the **mouse**.

Page Often used to mean a full screen of **data** as displayed by a **monitor**, though sometimes as with **Prestel**, each full screen is called a **frame** and a page consists of several frames. 'Paging' is the switching between blocks of computer memory and **radio-paging** is a British Telecom service.

Paper Tape Computer paper tape is usually $2\frac{1}{2}$ centimetres wide and comes in rolls 250 metres long. It is punched, one **character** at a time, with a row of holes; four rows per centimetre length. Each row has the same number of possible holes which can be 5, 6, 7 or 8. Eight-track tape is divided 5 to 3 by the **sprocket holes** which are punched at the same time and are used to guide the tape through the reader. Being off-centre the tape cannot be fed in upside down.

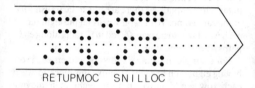

RETUPMOC SNILLOC

This type of coding can be read at 1500 characters per second by a paper tape reader.

Parallel Processing Conventional computers process data and instructions sequentially — they are brought in from central memory to the CPU, processed and then carried out. With parallel processing, microprocessors are wired in parallel, so processing takes place in many centres simultaneously. It is thought that this is how the human brain can do so many ordinary yet complex tasks. A cube of microprocessors together can deliver 40-50 m.i.p.s. (million instructions per second). This

151

is supercomputer performance housed in a micro. Applications requiring such power include weather forecasting and gigantic number-crunching operations. At present, the leading parallel processor is the INMOS Transputer.

Parallel Transmission This requires at least as many wires or paths as there are **bits** to be transmitted at the same time. With 8-bit **words** all the eight bits of each word would be transferred in parallel along eight paths at the same time.

For example: imagine six rows of soldiers each row having eight men in each. To move this block forward each row could move in turn, eight men moving 'parallel' to one another.

Alternatively the man at the left of each row could lead and his row could follow in line or 'serially':

In terms of electrical transmission this would require just one wire but in fact both systems would have parity checks and **handshake**.

Parameter Often in the course of carrying out a **program** (or a procedure) the computer does different tasks depending on the value of something or on the particular key that was last pressed. Such values which have a particular meaning to the computer are called parameters.

Parity Bit This extra bit is included with a set of **binary digits** as a check to see that all the binary digits are transferred correctly. Its value is 0 or 1 depending on the values of the other digits. If the number of 1's, including the parity bit, is even then the word has even parity; if the number of 1's is odd then it has odd parity.

153

Pascal Blaise Pascal (1623–1662), a French philosopher, mathematician and physicist who designed and built in 1642 a toothed gear-wheel machine that could do both addition and subtraction; the first mechanical **calculator**. Also Pascal is the name of a high-level programming language developed in the early 1970s as a teaching language. Today it is used for general purpose programming.

Password A group of **characters** correctly given when demanded by a computer allows access by the user.

PC Abbreviation for **Personal Computer**.

PCB Abbreviation for **Printed Circuit Board**.

PC-DOS A popular **operating system** for use on microcomputers.

Peripheral A device that can be connected and controlled by a computer but external to the CPU.

For example: a **card reader**, a disk drive, a **bar code** reader, **joysticks, paddles** and **visual display units** (VDU's).

154

Personal Computer (PC) A relatively powerful microcomputer normally used by one person. Smaller than the mainframe computer which can be used by several people at the same time, it is more powerful than a home computer and can use operating systems and business software as well as games software.

Pilot A computer programming language specifically designed for creating **computer-assisted learning** (CAL) packages. It has fourteen simple commands allowing the author to create sets of questions with routing for the student depending on the answers given.

PIO Abbreviation for Programmable **Input/Output**.

Pixel These are the tiny areas (dots or PICture ELements) that make up a computer graphics picture. The smaller each pixel, the greater their number and the higher the resolution of the picture (more detail can be seen). However the variation in brightness and the number of colours depend on the **bits** per pixel:

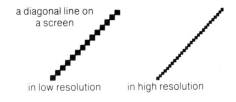

a diagonal line on a screen

in low resolution   in high resolution

For example, on a **monitor screen** 640 by 250 pixels may allow only four colours, whereas 320 by 250 pixels might allow sixteen colours.

PL/M Abbreviation for Programming Language for Microcomputers, an adapted version of **PL/1**.

PL/1 A **high-level language** designed with the intention of combining the problem solving facilities of **FORTRAN** with the **data**-handling capabilities of **COBOL**.

Plotter An instrument for drawing lines on paper, often used to draw the two-dimensional graphic output from a computer. On some instruments the pen is able to move in two directions; on others the pen moves in one direction and the paper is moved at right angles. Another method is to have the paper fixed to a cylinder which is able to revolve back and forwards while the pen moves sideways. Movement is generally done by *stepping motors*. Colour is achieved by using several (say four) different coloured pens, the carrier which moves selecting the right pen at the right time.

X-Y type Here the values of X and Y positions are fed by the computer to the plotter as coordinates which are plotted by the pens.

Incremental type As opposed to an X-Y plotter which requires X and Y values, this unit plots or draws according to **data** supplied by the computer, which moves it from its current position. Each plot is therefore relative to the previous plot and not to a fixed origin.

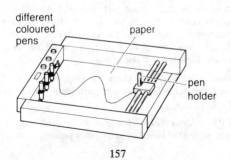

Other devices allow the paper holder to move back
and forth in one direction and the pen to move at right
angles. A *drum plotter* has the paper fixed to a drum
which rotates back and forth:

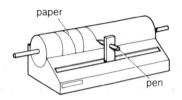

Point-of-Sale (POS) In a shop this is the place
where the goods change hands. When you pay at the
till the item becomes yours and any record, such as a
stock control figure, needs to be changed. A point-of-
sale **terminal** may have its own backing store
(magnetic cassette tape for example) or may be
directly connected to a computer. See also **Electronic
Funds Transfer at Point of Sale**.

Port The **integrated circuit**, or chip, which allows
the computer to **interface** with **peripherals**. See **User
Port**.

PPM Abbreviation for Pages Per Minute, a
measure of the speed of output of a **printer**.

Prestel The name of British Telecom's **viewdata** service designed for the home market with use during the evenings and weekends when telephone lines are under-used. At present, though, it is mainly used by business. Signals travel from one of the Prestel computers (all of which are linked) via telephone to a television screen. Nearly 200,000 different pages are available and these cover topics as wide apart as the selection of wines and British Rail train timetables. Information Providers (IP's) buy pages to display their goods or **information**. Users have to pay both telephone line charge and computer time charge when using the system and may also have to pay a page charge which is collected by British Telecom for the Information Providers. Most pages however have a zero page charge and it is possible to access other private viewdata systems through Prestel. Some pages consist of computer **software** and by connecting British Telecom approved **microcomputers** via approved MODEMS one can access this **tele-software**.

Printed Circuit Board (PCB) A thin board on which electronic components are fixed by solder. Often the component wires are pushed through from one side and soldered on the other side which has the printed circuit. The printed circuit consists of metal strips which connect one component to another. Several such boards might be used in a **micro-computer**, one having the **microprocessor**, another having sets of memory **chips** and others for **high resolution graphics**, controlling the disk drives and so on. Such a set of boards might all plug into a **mother-board** or be connected by a cable with many wires.

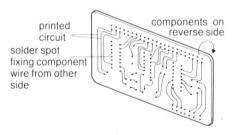

printed circuit

components on reverse side

solder spot fixing component wire from other side

Note that many more intricate connections are possible with a printed circuit board than with a wired circuit. In fact double-sided printed circuit boards are also available.

Printer This device or **peripheral** is used to obtain **hard copy** of the output from a computer. It can be either a mechanical, or impact, printer or a non-impact printer. Impact printers include **dot matrix**, chain, band, belt, thimble, or **daisywheel** machines. They are noisier and slower but have the advantage of being able to produce carbon copies while they print. Non-impact printers use thermal, **electrostatic, laser, ink-jet** or magnetic techniques. They are better suited for graphics work, although some impact printers can also output them. The most popular printers at the moment are dot matrix and daisywheels. The relative speeds of some printers are:

teleprinter	10–30 cps
daisywheel printer	50 cps
dot matrix printer	80 cps
ink-jet printer	200 cps
line printer	1000 lpm
xerographic laser printer	20 ppm

(cps=characters per second, lpm=lines per minute and ppm=pages per minute).

Program This is the set of **instructions** which the computer carries out. In whatever **language** the program is written the machine follows the instructions one at a time in order. There are five main steps in writing a program:

1) Understanding and solving the problem

2) Flowchart or plan of the solution
3) Coding the program
4) Writing the documentation
5) Trials for testing

With a **top down** approach to **structured programming** the first three steps would be applied to sections at a time resulting in a set of programs each having a particular problem to solve.

Program Counter   See **Control Register**.

Programmable Read Only Memory (PROM)
This is similar to a ROM **chip** whose non-**volatile memory** is used to store a fixed program. Using a special **hardware** device it is possible to create one's own ROM using a PROM, but unlike an **EPROM** it cannot then be changed.

Programmed Learning   The theory that self-study at one's own rate is possible and that direction to the next piece of work can be based on the results or answers to the questions of the previous piece. Never very widely used as a conventional scheme, computers have brought the student the advantage of an interactive medium capable of storing the progress made and presenting the right piece of work at the right time. **Computer-managed learning** (CML) is proving very successful for training in both commerce and industry and with a record-keeping element is doing much to assist our educational system.

Programming Language This is the language that allows the computer user to tell the computer what to do. There are many different languages some of which are mentioned in this book. Under the general heading of **high-level languages** one might include **ALGOL, FORTRAN, COBAL, BASIC** and **Pascal**. **Machine code** or the manufacturer's **assembler** would be **low-level languages**.

PROM Acronym for **Programmable Read Only Memory**.

Prompt The way in which the computer gives its operator a message. It may be a symbol (e.g. >), a sentence on a screen or a coloured light on the keyboard.

Pseudo-Random Sequence of Numbers When the computer is asked to generate a **random number** it does so by carrying out a set of **instructions**. The numbers produced can be taken as being random but it is possible to repeat the process starting in the same way and to obtain the same set of random numbers. Only if one can involve some other changing factor, such as the 'time' since switching on, can this partly be overcome.

PSS Abbreviation for Packet Switch Stream. See **Data Communications**.

p-Type The way in which a **semiconductor** such as **silicon** conducts electricity can be changed greatly by adding a small amount of an impurity. Some impurities such as phosphorus have a lack of electrons ('p' means more positive) and this gives us p-type silicon. Transistors are made by combining p-type and **n-type** materials together.

Punched Card Made of thin card this is used to store **data** which is read by detecting the positions of the holes that have been punched. The most common card has eighty columns and measures about eighteen centimetres by eight centimetres. There are twelve punching positions in each column and, generally, one particular hole is used for the digits 0 to 9 and a combination of two holes for the other **characters**. A few card codes use three holes in one column.

For example: the eighty-column card which uses the twelve-bit **Hollerith** code:

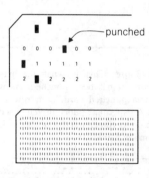

The ninety-six-column card is in fact smaller than the eighty-column card and uses round holes rather than rectangular ones. Designed for use in small businesses it can hold about 20 per cent more data:

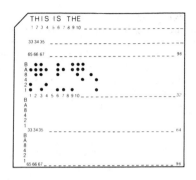

Punched Tape This is what the **paper tape** becomes after it has been punched. As with each column on a **punched card**, each row stores one **character**. A paper tape punch driven by a computer can punch up to 100 characters per second.

For example: 5-track tape.

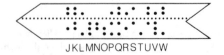

JKLMNOPQRSTUVW

As there are only thirty-two possible ways of punching

five holes a letter code punch (all five holes punch) precedes a section of tape with letters and a figure code punch precedes all other characters. In this way ten of the punching combinations can be used for both letters and numbers.

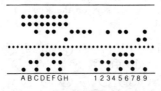

8-track tape

Note that this 8-track code has an odd-**parity bit**. The fourth row is a check row and is punched (or not) so as to make the number of holes punched in a row (or **frame**) odd.

Quad A **word** that uses 8 bytes. As a word is 2 bytes, equal to 16 bits, a quad is equal to 64 bits.

QWERTY This is used to describe the keyboard on a normal two-handed typewriter. The word comes from the first six keys on the second row of the keyboard.

It is interesting to note that the layout of the keys was designed not for speed as we might wish today, but for the opposite. Letters used often were positioned so as to allow time for the hammer to fall back to its place without being hit by the hammer of the next **character**.

Radio-Paging A service offered by British Telecom which allows the wearer of the device to be paged by someone who just dials a particular telephone number. The device does no more than 'beep' but it draws to the wearer's attention that someone wishes to make contact. Similar devices have been used by hospital doctors, firemen and factory foremen for some time.

Random Access Memory (RAM) This is a set of storage **locations** any of which can be accessed directly without having to work through from the first one. Such memories can both be written to and read from, and access times are about the same for all locations. RAM is a volatile memory: all is lost when power is switched off.

We tend to think of **semiconductor** memories as being the equivalent RAM to **core store**, though moving **magnetic memories** such as **disk** and drum are also RAM but have greater access times. Semiconductor RAM can be based on the **junction transistor** or the **field-effect transistor** (TTL or CMOS). The first offers the faster access but the latter offers both dynamic RAM and static RAM with dynamic being the cheaper but requiring extra logic circuits to check the contents regularly.

Random Numbers A set of numbers each one picked entirely at random. However this is not truly possible with most machines and we talk of a **pseudo-random sequence of numbers** as being produced by a **microcomputer**.

Read Only Memory (ROM) A **memory** that holds **data** or **instructions** permanently and cannot be altered by the computer or programmer. The actual content of a ROM is fixed at the time of its manufacture (**PROM** is fixed using a special device by the user; **EPROM** can be changed with difficulty by the user).

For example: a **semiconductor** ROM can be used to store **BASIC** in a **microcomputer** or to store the control programs in pocket calculators and other hand-held devices.

Read/Write Memory As opposed to **read only memory** (ROM), this type of **memory** can be written into, as well as read. It might be **random access memory** (RAM) or a random access disk **file** but **serial access memory**, such as **bubble memory** and magnetic tape, would also be included.

Real Time Processing This is used to describe a computer system which accepts **data** and updates its records at that time (in real time) feeding back results almost immediately so it can influence the source of data. This is unlike a **point-of-sale backing store** which may only be accessed by the computer once a day.

For example: an airline booking system is accessed by remote **terminals**. On receiving a booking it checks that it is available and if so updates its records and confirms the acceptance. From that time other users will find that booking is not available.

Re-Boot   A term instructing the user to **bootstrap** the system again. Often used when the **program** has gone wrong or is in an endless loop from which it cannot leave. Also used as a way of changing the program stored in a **microcomputer**; re-boot and re-load.

Red, Green, Blue (RGB)   A **video** signal system which uses these three colours to produce higher definition images than can be achieved with a single signal.

Reduced Instruction Set Computer   See **RISC**.

Register   A special type of store **location** in a computer used for a specific purpose. Generally registers are one or two **word**-lengths of the computer.

For example: one register might be used as the **accumulator**; another as the **store** address register.

Remote Control   At present such devices are used to operate television receivers, video recorders and some **Prestel** sets. Using a weak, infrared beam (like a light beam but one that is not detected by our eyes) these gadgets enable a person to operate the machine from various distances with a hand-held keypad. In a similar way one could operate a computer from the comfort of an armchair.

Remote Job Entry (RJE)   In **batch processing** the programs that have to be put into the computer may be entered at the computer site or from a number of remote sites. Remote job entry refers to the latter case.

Re-Run   To **run** the computer **program** again with the original **data** starting from the beginning.

Reserved Word   This is generally a **word** which has a specific meaning to the **compiler** and thus must not be used by the programmer when programming in the **high-level language**.

Response Time The time taken for a computer to answer after the last key is pressed. This time would be very short in the case of a **microcomputer** but varies greatly when accessing a **mainframe** computer from a **terminal**. The time includes transmission in both directions and would depend on the number of other users. Response time for **multi-access processing** systems should be within five seconds.

RGB Abbreviation for **Red, Green, Blue**.

Right Justification This is the arranging of lines of text so as to **justify** the right-hand edges and make them all in line. However it can also refer to **data** stored in consecutive locations all of which have been filled from the right and may have a different number of spaces on the left.

Right Shift In this operation all the **characters** in a particular **string** are moved one place to the right. If a number is involved then this would have the effect of division. For example, just as shifting a denary number one place to the right has the effect of dividing by ten so a binary number is divided by two:

in denary   768.0   becomes 76.8
in binary   11010 (=26)   becomes 1101 (=13)

173

RISC (Reduced Instruction Set Computer) It is reckoned that for most users 80 percent of their time is spent using only 20 percent of the microprocessor's instruction set. It makes sense, therefore, to have a computer with a microprocessor that has only the most frequently used instructions programmed in. These fundamental instructions are then used as building blocks and combined to form more complex tasks. The aim of keeping these building blocks straightforward, simple and easy is to obtain the maximum speed at which an instruction can be executed. RISCs have speeds of three m.i.p.s. (million instructions per second) and upwards. This contrasts with **CISC** microprocessors where complexities result in slowness of operation.

RISC microprocessors can also **emulate** instruction sets of different computers. Existing software will run many times faster, and it is easy to port (transfer) high-level languages like Pascal and C across many different computers.

Examples of RISCs include Acorn Archimedes, IBM PC-RT. RISC technology is becoming an important development in microprocessors.

RJE Abbreviation for **Remote Job Entry**.

Robotics The linking of electronics and **micro-**

electronics with machines, including cameras, enables complicated and repetitive tasks to be done automatically without human involvement. As machines become more 'intelligent' so more intricate work can be carried out.

Rogue Value   When **data**, such as a series of numbers, is being put into a computer a rogue value is given at the end to show that there are no more numbers.

For example: when putting in a set of values which are the ages in years of a group of people the value 999 might be used as the rogue value. It must not be possible for the rogue value to appear as one of the set.

ROM   Acronym for **Read Only Memory**.

Rounding   This is one way of reducing a number to a certain number of digits. In **denary notation** if the last digit removed from the right-hand side is a 5 or above the last figure remaining is increased by one.

For example: rounding the number 672.87 to four figures would give 672.9; rounding to three figures would give 673; to two figures would give 670. On the other hand **truncation** to four figures would give 672.8.

Routine   This refers to a piece of **software** that does a specific task though generally it is also part of a **program**. However the word **subroutine** is often used to describe a self-contained section of a program.

RS232, RS423   Standard interfaces for **serial transmission** of data. See also **Data Communications**.

Run   Often this word is used as a command to tell the computer to carry out a program though it can imply the loading, the execution and the output of a whole package. The 'run-time' is a measure of the time taken for the whole program to be carried out.

Scheduling This is the arranging of the order in which programs are to be run and may be done by the computer itself.

For example: it may not be possible to run the first program in a queue if it requires more memory than is available at that time. Even programs that are running sometimes let others go ahead if a certain **peripheral**, say a **printer**, is not free when required.

Schema This word refers to an outline description or diagram of a **database** that can be accessed by the computer.

Scratch Pad Memory Just as we might use a scratch pad for working out, say, the cost of 24 pens at 17p each so the computer may reserve an area of **memory** for holding results of calculations that it will need later.

Screen This is the front of a television set, **visual display unit** (VDU) or **monitor** and is used for displaying computer text and graphics.

   Screen copy refers to the output from a computer as seen on a screen;

   Screen editor refers to the editing facilities offered to the user by a **terminal** screen; and

   screen memory refers to the memory available to the computer or the user in the terminal itself.

Scroll This is the continuous movement of the display on the **screen** where generally as one line is added at the bottom all lines move up one and the line at the top disappears from view. Most **microcomputers** can be set to scroll either one page at a time (one screenful) or continuously. Horizontal scrolling is used with some **word processors**. Here, should the line length be greater than the screen width then on reaching the right-hand side of the screen the whole display moves to the left. Some **text editor** type programs only move the particular line to the left.

Search Whereas it would be far too time consuming for us to search a large set of records for particular items this is in fact one thing that a computer can do very quickly. In a search, each item would be accessed and checked in turn by the program which would only select those required.

Second Generation Computers These computers built between the mid 1950s and the mid 1960s used transistors. Thus they were smaller, more reliable and required less power than the **first generation computers** which used electronic **valves**.

Second Generation Languages (2GL) These came about with the advent of transistors and are a step up from programming in machine code. 2GLs allow you to program using a function code (sometimes called a mnemonic, or memory aid) and a location showing where to find the data. Such languages became known as **assembly languages**. They depend on the type of CPU used, are tedious to program but are quickly converted and executed (run) by the assembler (translator). Examples:

function code	*location*	
LDA	100	(load accumulator with contents of location 101)
ADD	101	(add contents of location 101)
STO	102	(store answers in location 102)

Sector A magnetic **disk** or drum uses circular tracks for storing **data**. These tracks are **format**ted into

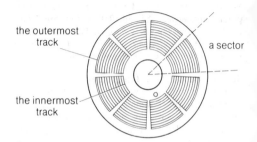

the outermost track

a sector

the innermost track

sectors and the computer writes data, one sector track at a time, from its memory. Note that although the length of a track in a sector near the centre of a **mini-floppy disk** is shorter it holds the same amount of data as those further out.

Seed Crystal This is a small single crystal which when held in its own supersaturated solution grows into a large crystal.

For example: a small **silicon** seed crystal is rotated and slowly withdrawn from molten silicon to give the cylindrical crystal from which silicon **wafers** are cut.

180

Segment Display   Used with **light-emitting diodes** and **liquid-crystal displays** to show the numbers 0 to 9. Generally the seven segments, a, b, c, d, e, f and g, lean slightly to the right:

The patterns are:

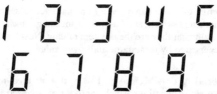

Segmented Program   This is a computer **program** written in sections which are called up from **backing store** as and when required. One section would probably **overlay** the previous section in the **main store**.

Semiconductor This is a material which is neither a good conductor of electricity like copper nor a good insulator like plastic. It is somewhere between the two and the way in which it conducts electricity can be changed by adding (called 'doping') a small amount of another substance (an impurity).

For example: **silicon** is a semiconductor; doping it with a small amount of arsenic provides extra negative electrons giving what is known as **n-type** silicon; doping with phosphorus provides a lack of electrons giving **p-type**. Other semiconductors include germanium and the compound gallium arsenide.

Sentinel The name given to a **character** or set of characters which have a special meaning which is usually that they are the last item of **data**. Now being superseded by **terminator** and **rogue value**.

Serial Access Memory This **read/write memory** is a set of **locations** which can only be accessed in sequence.

For example: to read a particular record stored on a magnetic tape it would be necessary to go through all the records in sequence until is is found. Another example is **bubble memory** though here **access times** would be shorter.

Serial Transmission   This method is where each **character** or piece of **data** is transmitted in order, one after the other along a wire rather than having one wire for each bit as in **parallel transmission**. Certain standard interfaces have been defined for serial ports and these include RS232, V24 and RS423.

Seven-Segment Display   See **Segment Display**.

Shared Files   These are files held in the **immediate access store** of a computer acting as a file server or in **backing store**, which can be read, used and altered by other computers.

Shift Register   This is a **location** in the computer which is used only for shifting **data** to the left or right. Note that a shift one place to the left on a denary number is like multiplying by ten, though the first digit of the number is lost if it filled the location completely.

For example, with a denary number:

0	4	7	2

Shift left is like multiplying by 10:

4	7	2	0

Shift right is like dividing by 10:

0	0	4	7

In **binary notation**:

| 0 | 1 | 1 | 0 | (=6)
|---|---|---|---|

Shift left is like multiplying by 2:

| 1 | 1 | 0 | 0 | (=12)
|---|---|---|---|

Shift right is like dividing by 2:

| 0 | 0 | 1 | 1 | (=3)
|---|---|---|---|

Signal This is a way of using electricity to convey **data** along a cable or through an electronic system. The change may be in the current flowing or the voltage used. In an analogue signal the change can have any value but with a digital signal there are only two values (interpreted as a 0 or 1).

For example: a common standard for serial transmission is RS232C where a 0 is less than −6 volts and a 1 is greater than +6 volts.

Sign Bit With eight-**bit** words usually seven bits are used to represent the number and the eighth, the sign: 0 for positive and 1 for negative. In the commonly used **two's complement** notation only the first digit is negative and this indicates the sign.

For example:

| 0 1000001 | would be +65 |

| 1 0011011 | would be −101 |

In **floating-point arithmetic** a second eight-bit word for each number would give the position of the 'bicimal'point.

Silicon A cheap and widely available **semi-conductor** material that has replaced germanium in most electronic **solid state devices**. Although it is the second most abundant element (after oxygen) on the Earth's surface it does not occur naturally. Sand and quartz are natural forms of silica (silicon dioxide) from which silicon is obtained.

Silicon Disk Also known as RAM disk, this is an extra RAM (**random access memory**) card which when inserted into the computer acts as a fast **disk** drive. A **utility** program is used to set up links to the CPU and modify the RAM area. Using a silicon disk can speed up, by at least five times or more, the loading, saving and operation of application packages. For some software silicon disk is an essential requirement, particularly for those that use up memory very quickly.

Simplex Operation   Unlike **duplex operation** this mode of transmission allows **data** to travel in only one direction. A terminal that communicates with a computer via such a channel can either send or receive but not both. Duplex allows travel in both directions at the same time; half-duplex allows travel in both directions but not at the same time.

For example: simplex transmission could be from the **keyboard** of a **terminal** to its computer 'or' from the computer to the **visual display unit** screen of the terminal.

Simulation   The representation or modelling of a situation by a computer system to ensure that the decisions and actions of the user cause the same effects and results as when carried out for real. This mode of use of a computer assists training, particularly where mistakes in the real situation would be too costly or too dangerous.

For example: learning to fly a helicopter or operating a nuclear power station.

Small-Scale Integration (SSI)   See **Large-Scale Integration**.

Smartcard   A new form of plastic, the size of a credit card. This type has a silicon chip embedded in a corner, storing up to 64 Kilobytes of data and instructions. The chip can communicate and store bank account, credit/money transactions and personal details. A machine can be used to read and record data on to the chip. Any misuse of the card can be indicated and **stored**, resulting in card failure. The smartcard has been extensively tested in France and the USA and is expected to be in worldwide use in the 1990s.

The smartcard contrasts with the **lasercard** which has a silver surface on which data is burnt as a series of dips.

Soft-Sectored   This describes the way in which the length of a **sector** is fixed on a **floppy disk**. In this case the length is set by the **microcomputer** when the disk is **format**ted. Soft-sectored floppy disks are distinguished from **hard-sectored** ones by the fact that they have only a single hole near the centre hole of the disk (hard-sectored have a ring of say 6 or 12).

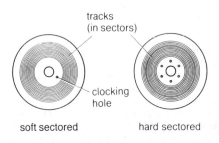

soft sectored   hard sectored

Softstrip A new paper data-storage method. Data is coded in **binary** as complex vertical black and white patterns on a strip of paper 24 centimetres long and 16 millimetres wide. Up to 5.5 Kilobytes of data, in up to ten files, can be held on a full length strip. Approximately 40 Kilobytes could be held on a sheet of A4 paper.

Programs, languages, text and graphics can be encoded on to the paper strip, using a stripmaking program. Softstrips can be photocopied and sent through the post as well as distributed through magazines.

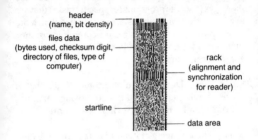

Data can be read by an infra-red scanner. This means that tea/coffee and other stains have no detrimental effect. If the strip is scribbled over, however, then reading cannot take place.

The advantages of softstrip are low cost and portability. It is a good way of distributing data instead of using vast amounts of ordinary paper. It is at present being used in the USA for computer magazine (public domain software), mailing lists and database distribution. Data distributed by this method is becoming known as *stripware*.

189

Software   Software, as opposed to **hardware**, refers to all the **programs** that can be run on a particular computer. It would include the **operating system**, the **assemblers**, the **compilers** and all the software packages (specific programs for specific tasks) that are available. Software houses are companies that write and supply software packages for computer systems; thus one does not have to buy all software from the computer manufacturer.

Solid State Device   An electronic device that is made of solid material and has no moving parts.
For example: **transistors**, **chips**, **core store**.

Sort   The arranging of items of **data** (a **file** of names or types of product say) into a predetermined order. This might be alphabetic or **numeric** such as house number or date order. Sorting may be carried out on the whole file (thus every entry is then stored in sequence) or may be done only on those items selected for printing. A computer sorts by comparing the items of data, two at a time and exchanging their positions in memory if necessary. Different methods of sorting (e.g. bubble sort, shell sort) make the comparisons in different orders and sometimes the sort is only carried out on part of the record. **Inverted files** are sorted on a particular part of each record and although the sorting (*file inversion*) is very time consuming, in use such files are quickly accessed.

Source Language   This is the language in which the programmer writes his **program** (the *source program*) though it cannot be directly understood by a computer. Either the source program is converted to an **object** program (**machine code** which can be run directly by the computer) using a **compiler** or it is run one line at a time using an **interpreter**.

For example: **BASIC, COBOL, ALGOL** are all examples of source languages.

Speech Recognition   This is the interpretation by a computer of the spoken word. Already in use are machines that respond to words though the vocabulary is limited and the pronunciation must be clear. Development at present is limited by processor speeds and memory sizes.

Speech Synthesizer   This is the generation of speech by **solid state** circuits. Used in hand-held educational machines and toys where a limited vocabulary is required. At present there is a noticeable difference between machine and human speech but more variation in machine accent is becoming available.

Spreadsheet This is a screen-based representation of a large sheet of paper on which data can be manipulated to produce calculations at the touch of a button. The screen is divided into rows and columns, each intersection containing a cell. Data and strings as headings can be entered. By devising your own formula rules, individual cells can be chained together to produce results. A cell change will automatically trigger a chain of revised calculations.

Because of the computer's manipulative ability, spreadsheets are useful for problem-solving strategies and modelling of real-life events. Sometimes called 'what if' situations, spreadsheets can show the effects of changing events, circumstances, costs, etc to the final results. Example:

	A		B		C		D		E		F		G		H		I		J
1									UNIT	TOTAL		UNIT	TOTAL					
2	ITEM		PRICE		DISC		SALES		REV	REVENUE		COST	COST		PROFIT		PER CENT
3			£		%				£	£		£	£		£		%
4	Pens		1.50		40		745		.90	670.50		.33	245.85		424.65		63.33
5			1.55		40		667		.93	620.31		.34	226.78		393.53		63.44
6			1.60		40		531		.96	509.76		.35	185.85		323.91		63.54
7	Clip pencils		1.25		40		830		.75	622.50		.27	224.10		398.40		64.00
8			1.35		40		775		.81	627.75		.28	217.00		410.75		65.43
9			1.45		40		689		.87	599.43		.29	199.81		399.62		66.67
10	A4 paper		1.35		40		927		.81	750.87		.30	278.10		472.77		62.96
11			1.45		40		824		.87	716.88		.31	255.44		461.44		64.37
12			1.50		40		732		.90	658.80		.32	234.24		424.56		64.44
13	A3 paper		1.55		40		597		.93	555.21		.35	208.95		346.26		62.37
14			1.60		40		523		.96	502.08		.36	188.28		313.80		62.50
15			1.65		40		412		.99	407.88		.37	152.44		255.44		62.63
16	A5 paper		1.00		40		995		.60	597.00		.25	248.75		348.25		58.33
17			1.15		40		836		.69	576.84		.26	217.36		359.48		62.32
18			1.30		40		774		.78	603.72		.27	208.98		394.74		65.38

Sprocket Holes These appear as a series of holes along punched paper tape and along the edges of **continuous stationery**. In both cases they are used to feed the item automatically through a device.

For example: paper tape.

SSI Abbreviation for **Small-Scale** Integration. See **Large-Scale Integration**.

Stack A temporary area of **memory** used to hold sets of **data**. As each item is added the previous ones are all shifted down one place — thus they are thought of as being 'stacked' one above the other. New items are added at the end and only the end one can be removed at any time (i.e. last in first out).

Stationery Computer stationery is usually of the **continuous stationery** type which consists of fan-folded pages joined by perforations and having **sprocket holes** along the edges. These forms may be pre-printed with the name of the company or organization, leaving space on each page for the computer print. Sets of single sheets can be printed using single-sheet feeders.

Stepping Motor As opposed to an ordinary electric motor this turns a step at a time with, say, 96 steps for one revolution. The number of steps is fixed by the manufacturer and depends on both the number of sets of coils and the number of coils in each set. With 4 sets each having 12 coils, 48 positions are possible and 96 steps can be achieved by holding half-way between positions. It is moved from one position to the next by activating different sets of coils in turn, using a sequence of numbers which can be provided by the digital **output** of a computer. This is an important method of producing precise movement under **microprocessor** control and is widely used in **robotics**.

Store This is the name given to anything that can retain **data** given to it by the **central processing unit** of a computer. **Core store,** memory **chips**, **bubble memory**, magnetic **disk**, drum and **tape** are all types of store. The size of a store depends on the number of memory locations.

String Bearing in mind the old adage 'How long is a piece of string?' the computer uses this word to describe a set of **characters** which may in fact only be one character. Whereas numbers are stored in fixed length memories, the spaces being filled with zeros, characters are used in groups of various lengths. They are stored in a series of memory **locations** with the first location holding a number giving the length of the string (the number of characters). BASIC uses the dollar ($) symbol next to the **variable** to denote that it is a string.

For example: A$='HELLO' and this word might be stored in six locations, the first holding the number 5.

Stripware The term given to data stored or distributed on **softstrip**.

Structured Programming This is the art of writing **programs** that are logical and easy to follow. It involves the sectioning of the original problem into small program units each of which is self-contained and can be tested separately. The main program can then consist of a series of **instructions** each sending the computer to a particular unit or **subroutine** which it carries out and then returns. In addition instructions such as FOR... NEXT, REPEAT... UNTIL and DO ... WHILE ... allow easy structuring in program writing. With a **top down** approach the program is written in units in the same way as the problem was originally solved and it can be argued that **flowcharts**

are not required with this method. However the programming needs to be extremely well structured to work first time without them.

Subroutine   This is a section of a **program** written to carry out a specific task which the main program may use just once or several times during its run. The last **instruction** of a subroutine usually returns the computer to the instruction following the one from which it left the main program. Large computer systems have a set of subroutines on disk or tape which can be 'called' and used by the current program as and when required. A 'procedure' is a form of subroutine in that the programmer can use it once or several times during a program. The main difference is that it is 'called' by name and must be defined (written) outside the main body of the program. It can also have its own **variables**.

Synchronous Mode   This is the performance of a computer whereby the start of every operation is dependent on a pulse from its internal clock. Thus the completion of one task does not signal the start of the next as in **asynchronous mode** — the machine waits, albeit for a fraction of a second, for the next clock pulse.

Syntax   Just as the words we speak need to be in a certain grammatical order to be understood so the **instructions** to a computer must obey certain rules. 'Syntax error' is stated by the machine when instruction errors have been made by the programmer.

For example: the instruction

10 INPUT A;B

in BASIC would give a syntax error because it should be

10 INPUT A,B

and the rules for writing program instructions have not been obeyed.

System   This is the total of all the things that make up the working computer unit. It includes **hardware** (the computer itself plus all the **peripheral** units), **software** and the necessary **data** and operators.

System Analysis   This is the evaluation coupled if necessary with the design and installation of a computer system to solve a problem. Several stages are involved:

1) Analysis of how the job is done at present.
2) Deciding if a computer can be of use.
3) Breaking down the problem into logical steps, designing a solution and specifying exactly what the computer must do.
4) Installing the computer system and seeing it works as required.

System Flowcharts Used by systems analysts to understand, design and pinpoint the flow of work in a computer system. The flowchart can be used in planning and specifying particular programs that need developing. See also **Flowcharts**.

Examples of system signs:

magnetic tape magnetic disk visual display unit

document punched card paper tape

manual input keyboard   communications link

System X   The name of British Telecom's digital **telecommunications** system. Speech from a telephone is converted into digital **data** (0's and 1's) and these digital signals are transmitted, as opposed to the continuously varying analogue **signals** as at present. Such signals can also be sent via **fibre optics** cables.

Table In science work, results from experiments are sometimes recorded in a table of values. Temperature and time readings as a liquid cools might be listed in two columns:

Temperature/C	Time/s
72	0
60	30
51	60
44	90
38	120
33	150

Such results could be stored as an **array** in a computer memory as:

(72,0) (60,30) (51,60) (44,90)   and so on.

This arrangement of **data** in rows and columns is called a table. In addition items in such a table can be easily located by means of a **look-up table** which directs the computer without its having to search every item.

Tabulator The name given to the calculating equipment available from 1890 to about 1960. **Hollerith** built the first tabulator which read and counted the 1890 USA census figures from **punch cards**. Others could be programmed by making wire connections between holes on a control panel.

Tape   A long strip of paper or magnetic coated plastic which is used to record **data**. **Paper tape** can use 5, 6, 7 or 8 holes to represent each **character** and half-inch magnetic tape similarly uses 7 or 9 channels across its width. (Audio cassette tape records **bits** serially one after the other.) One difference with magnetic tape is that data is usually stored in blocks and that in addition to checking the **parity bit** of each character the computer checks each block as it is read.

Tbyte   Abbreviation for **Tetrabyte**.

Telecommunications   The sending of **data** from one place to another by radio waves or cables. Note the derivative of this word in the title 'British Telecom'.

Teleprinter   Teleprinters and teletypewriters are devices similar to typewriters.

Teleprinters were originally designed to send and receive messages transmitted serially using a telephone line and a 5-**bit** code.

Teletypewriters usually work with the 8-bit **ASCII code** and are used specifically for sending and receiving messages to and from computer systems.

Both can have a tape reader and punch attached so that tapes can be prepared **off line** and read at a later time. As an **output** device they usually work at 10 or 30 characters per second and suitably adapted they make a cheap but slow secondhand printer for a **microcomputer**.

Telesoftware This describes the transmission of computer **software** from one computer to another by **telecommunications**. At present telesoftware is available on both the BBC's and IBA's **teletext** services and British Telecom's **Prestel** system, though radio transmissions are also being tried. **Ceefax** page 700 onwards, **Oracle** page 175 onwards and Prestel, details given on page 2114.

Teletext An information service transmitted as part of the normal television signal. Each page is transmitted in turn in a never-ending sequence as a form of 'dots' tucked away out of sight at the top of the television screen. If the receiving set is fitted with a teletext decoder these top four lines of the picture can be made to fill the whole screen. The user selects the page number and that page is decoded the next time it is transmitted. Information available varies from pages on news and sport to food prices and film reviews. IBA's version of teletext is called **Oracle** and the BBC's is called **Ceefax**. Uses of teletext now include advertising, local information and **tele-software**.

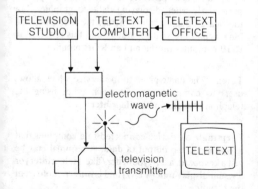

Television Receiver   This is the television set most people have in their home. It normally receives a transmitted signal via an aerial or cable and converts this radio frequency (RF) signal (or more precisely UHF signal) into picture plus colour and sound. Most **microcomputers** have a socket which gives a signal suitable for displaying the **output** on a television receiver but it is necessary to 'tune' the set to the required channel the first time this is done. Some sets are receiver/**monitor** and these have a second input socket which accepts a **video** signal from a microcomputer. This provides a better quality picture particularly when displaying detailed graphics. For the clearest quality colour picture the **red, green** and **blue** signals are sent separately and this requires an RGB computer output and an RGB monitor.

Telex   The name given to the service which allows users to communicate with each other using the telephone system and a **teleprinter**.

Terminal   A device connected to a computer that allows input and output of **data**. A terminal may be just a keyboard, a teletypewriter (like a **teleprinter**) or a **visual display unit** (VDU) and is often remote from the computer.

For example: a magnetic stripe card reader, keyboard and display as in a bank cash dispenser or a bar code reader and cash till at a supermarket checkout.

An intelligent terminal has its own processing power, a dumb terminal has not.

Terminator   This, like a **rogue value**, is a false value attached to the end of a set of data and is used to indicate to the computer that it is the last item. Similarly, terminators are used on **punched tape** to indicate the end of each record.

Tetrabyte (Tbyte)   The term for 1000 **gigabytes**, or 1024 **megabytes**, or a staggering 1,073,741,824 **bytes**.

Text Editor   A piece of software often thought of as a limited **word processing** package. It can be used to create **files** of text, modify such files and **format** their layout prior to printing. In addition such software allows modification of the order and content of any set of **data** which the computer has created as part of a program. This is a useful way of quickly adding an item in the middle of a set of records thus moving all those below one step down.

Thin Film Memories This is the name of **integrated circuits (chips)** made by depositing thin layers in patterns on top of one another. The chips on **silicon wafers** are built a layer at a time, the pattern of each layer being governed by a particular mask. The process by which ultra-violet light is used to define the pattern and thus the circuit is called photo-lithography. Today X-ray radiation and electron beams are used to define the pattern as with their smaller wavelengths more circuits and thus more memories are possible on the same size chip. **Epitaxy** is another method being used with other **semi-conductors** to manufacture thin film memories.

Third Generation Computers These computers were the ones built using **integrated circuits**, the first in 1966. The second generation used **transistors** whilst the first generation used electronic **valves**.

Third Generation Languages (3GL) These are problem-solving languages and are not dependent on the type of CPU used, as were **second generation languages**. They came about with the introduction of integrated circuits and use commands/keywords which are near to English and have to be translated in machine code by either an **interpreter** or a **compiler**. These third generation languages (also known as high level languages) are good for general purpose programming, although some do specialize. They are widely used in education as well as for the development of code and they are portable across many computers.

Examples of 3GLs are:

COBOL for business uses
FORTRAN for scientific functions
Pascal and C for structure and file handling
Logo for list and database processing
BASIC for general purposes.

Time-Sharing This is the way in which two or more users seem to be using the computer at the same time. In fact the computer is dealing with each in turn but to the user it seems that they have sole use. **Output** to a **printer** for one user though, could be printed at the same time as the computer does a calculation for another user. Only when the number of time-sharing users becomes large does the delay become notice-able. See also **Multi-Access Processing System**.

Top Down This refers to one method of

programming whereby the programmer divides the problem into many small units each of which follows on from the one before. A computer **program** is then written for each of these units and tested separately. Only when it runs successfully is it added to the previous one. In this way the final program is built from the top downwards, and it is argued that no **flowchart** is required when using this method. However **structured programming** is required for easy understanding.

Trace   The name given to a piece of **software** which follows each step of a **program** line by line. It enables the user to check and locate errors in programs by printing each line number as it carries out that instruction.

Track   The name given to the channel or line along which **data** is recorded on a storage device.

For example: the row of holes on **paper tape** or the magnetic line parallel to the edge on magnetic tape.

Tractor Feed   The name given to the method of moving paper through a **printer** where it is held by the

sprocket holes along the two edges. The advantage over friction feed is that when using pre-printed **continuous stationery** the lining-up of the paper and print is far more accurate.

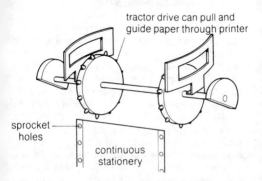

tractor drive can pull and guide paper through printer

sprocket holes

continuous stationery

For example: most small printers offer friction feed (the paper is held by the roller like a typewriter) but a tractor feed can be an optional extra.

Transducer Any device that converts energy *from* an electrical form or *to* an electrical form.

For example: a loudspeaker is a transducer in that it

converts electrical energy into sound energy that we can hear. Other examples include:

> A light sensitive pen in a bar code reader
> An electric motor
> An electrical thermometer

Transistor Invented in 1948 it revolutionized the electronic and computing world by replacing the unreliable **valve**. This **solid state** device is small, reliable, cheap and consumes very little power. It can be used as an amplifier or as a switching device, the latter forming the basis of computer logic and memory circuits. Joining two transistors together leads to **astable** and **bistable** circuits which are the building blocks of today's electronic systems. Transistors are made from **p-type** and **n-type** (n-p-n being the most common) **semiconductors** such as **silicon**, germanium and gallium arsenide. There are two main types of **transistor**, the **junction transistor** and the **field-effect transistor** (FET). The first type, sometimes known as 'bipolar', is the faster acting and more robust of the two though the voltage at which it works is more critical and a stabilized 5-volt power supply is required. The first **chip** was created in 1959 when a (junction) transistor and resistor were built together, hence the term *transistor-resistor-logic* or TRL.

Transistor-Transistor-Logic (TTL) The **logic circuit** design of joining the **junction** or bipolar transistor together on a **chip** has changed over the years from transistor-resistor-logic (TRL) in 1959 to TTL today. It is now used in the largest family of integrated circuits, the 7400 series, which has more than 100 different chips. However because of its need for a 5-volt stabilized power supply, it has been replaced in many applications by the other type, CMOS (based on the FET). These operate over a wider voltage range (3 to 15 volts), use less power and allow more logic gates per chip.

Tree This describes a non-linear method of storing **data** in a computer. One piece of data relates to several other pieces and each one of these then relates to more. The computer tree however is upside down with the branches spreading out downwards.

Note that ROGER can be accessed from the root

(Peter) as the third piece of data via PETER and STEPHEN. In fact all can be accessed within three. If the names were stored in alphabetical order ROGER would be the fifth piece of data accessed.

TRL Abbreviation for **Transistor**-Resistor-Logic.

Truncation When reducing the number of significant figures in a number, truncation, unlike **rounding**, involves their removal without any consideration of their value.

For example: truncation to three significant figures of the numbers 56.79 and 23820 would result in the loss of a 9 and 2 respectively:

> 56.79 would become 56.7
> 23820 would become 23800

Truth Table This is a table usually filled with 0's and 1's to show the changes carried out by logical operations such as **AND**, **OR**, **XOR**, and **NOT**.

an AND gate

For example: an AND gate only gives an output of
logical value 1 when all its inputs have a logical value
of 1. For a two input AND gate the truth table would
be:

Input		Output
0	0	0
0	1	0
1	0	0
1	1	1

TTL Abbreviation for **Transistor-Transistor-Logic**.

Turnkey Just as one would expect the door to open
on turning a key so a turnkey system for a
microcomputer is one that **bootstraps** and loads the
program automatically as soon as one switches on.

2GL See **Second Generation Language**.

Two's Complement A method of holding
negative numbers in **binary notation** so that they can
be added and subtracted. It also shows how negative
numbers are expressed.

In a binary number line, the most significant digit

(the last column from the right) indicates a positive or negative number whatever the length of the **word**.

−16	8	4	2	u

1	A 1 in that column indi-
Ø	cates a negative number. A Ø indicates a positive number.

Two's complement can also be used to find the negative form of a positive number or vice versa. The usual way of doing subtraction is for example:

$$7 - 5 = 2$$

The adding method of subtraction involves adding numbers to make the answer. Example:

What number when added to 5 equals 7? $5 + ? = 7$

Finding the negative form (or vice versa): what one is doing is answering the question, 'What number when added to the original sums to zero?' (in other words, that number indicates the opposite form). Example:

$$+5 -5 = 0$$
$$-23 +23 = 0$$

Opposite's method: find the one's complement (reverse all the digits) and add 1. Two's complement is sometimes called **negation** +1.

Number	One's complement (reverse all the digits)	Two's complement (one's complement +1)
0101 (= +5)	1010	1011 (= −5)
0100 (= +4)	1011	1100 (= −4)
1011 (= −5)	0100	0101 (= +5)

Doing subtraction: find the two's complement then add:

	find the opposite form	then add
0101 (=+5)	0101	0101
−0011 (+ 3) →	1101 (= −3) →	+1101
?		10010
		=0010

as we are working
in a 4-bit binary

(check 5−3 = 2)

UHF   Abbreviation for **Ultra High Frequency**.

ULA   Abbreviation for **Uncommitted Logic Array**.

Ultra High Frequency (UHF)   A particular range of radio waves having wavelengths approximately between 10 and 100cm. They are used for television transmissions and as **microcomputer** outputs which connect through the aerial socket for display on a **television receiver**. Frequency values are a few hundred million hertz.

Uncommitted Logic Array (ULA)   This is the name given to a **chip** on which there are sets of **logic circuits** that have not yet been connected together.

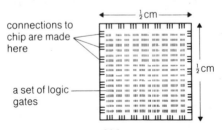

connections to chip are made here

a set of logic gates

216

Each set is complete in itself but has to be linked to the others by one or more connections. Thus a chip manufacturer makes his standard ULA which has the final layer (the circuit pattern) added according to the purchaser's specification. This enables the purchaser to obtain their own particular type of chip without the large expense of having one specially designed. See also **ASICS**.

Underflow This is the generation of a number, say by division, which is too small for the computer to store (the computer would in fact store zero). In **floating-point notation** using two 8-bit words this would happen when the resulting number was below 10^{-39}. That is a one over a one with thirty-nine noughts.

For example: on a 6-digit **calculator** dividing the number 0.000001 by 2 would give zero. Underflow is the name given when the right-hand digits are lost.

UNIVAC Acronym for UNIVersal Automatic Computer, the first commercial computer which was developed in 1951 by Remington Rand (now Sperry Univac).

UNIX A new **operating system** developed by Bell Laboratories. The **high-level language** C was designed for use with it.

Update   This describes the process of changing a file or program package so as to bring it up-to-date. This would include additions of new **data**, changes in data already held and alterations to the program to remove minor errors which have been found. The latter is sometimes called a 'patch'.

For example: an update may be necessary to a payroll package as a result of new Government legislation on PAYE (pay-as-you-earn income tax).

User Group   This is a group of people who meet or correspond regularly because of their interest in a particular machine. Most makes of **microcomputers** have their own user groups, generally supported by the manufacturer but controlled by the members. Meetings allow the sharing of both problems and solutions and provide advance information on new products. Much is to be gained at a small cost for all those who become members.

User Port   This is a socket with interface circuits behind it which allows the user to connect additional equipment to the computer. Often, but not always, it consists of eight **data** lines 'out' and eight 'in' plus particular voltage lines. Numbers that are sent appear in binary.

For example: in 8-**bits** the number 12 would appear

on the eight lines as 00001100 where a logical 0 would be 0 volts and a logical 1 between 4.5 and 5.0 volts.

A serial interface port is where data is transmitted serially, one after another. Example: RS232C, RS423 ports. A parallel interface port is where data is transmitted in parallel. Each bit has its own wire and all bits are transmitted together. Example, centronics port.

Utility Programs These are programs designed to perform particular tasks such as listing a **file** held on magnetic **tape** on the printer or copying **data** from one **disk** to another prior to a program run.

Validation Check This is a check that **data** is sensible, as mistakes can be made by the original data collector. Validation checks do not totally eliminate mistakes, but they make it difficult for wrong data to get through into the computer.

For coded numbers there are several methods:

Checksum digit: a coded number is summed and divided by a predetermined modulus. If the number can be divided exactly, i.e. there is no remainder, then the number is valid and sensible.

Weighted check digit: an extra stage of multiplying each digit by a factor is included. It is reckoned that it would be hundreds of years before a wrongly coded number got through.

Range checks: checks that the data is within accepted limits. Example:
IF age% < 1 OR age% > 1 THEN PRINT 'data error'.

Checks on number tables:
The use of **hash** (batch) **totals**. All the data in the table is summed to produce a nonsense total. This total is checked at the preparation and input stage.

Checks on strings (words/names/lists etc):
The use of **look-up** reference **tables** which are files of

data such as names, addresses, lists stored on disk. The computer compares and matches each entry against the data table.

All these validation checks can be programmed into the computer so it can carry out automatic checking.

Valve An electronic device created around 1900 in which electrodes are enclosed in glass (like a light bulb). Used in radios, television receivers and computers, the first computer had about 18,000 valves. The valve has now been largely replaced by the **transistor** and other **semiconductor** devices.

Variable This is a special store or memory area used when programming for holding data from the user. The data can be either entered from the keyboard or written into the program. A variable is so called because you can vary (change) data inside it. Each variable has a name and a type to identify it. Examples:

Common variable types in BASIC:
name% = integer (whole number) variable
name$ = string or text variable
name = real number variable (accepts decimal
                parts)

Using variables:

answer %: = first % + second %
PRINT carname$

This will display the contents of carname$.

If data is in the form of **strings** (strings of characters), several locations together might be used to hold the data.

VDU   Abbreviation for **Visual Display Unit**.

Verification   This is a check that something has been accurately typed and transmitted. It is the job of the inputter to type accurately what is before them, but mistakes can be made. For example, some typical mistakes in keying in 041772 could be:

1. Transcription error (a digit wrongly typed): 041792
2. Transposition (a pair of digits change place): 042771
3. Double transposition (double pairs change place): 014277
4. Random errors (complete mess)

Verification ensures such errors do not get through as mistakes can be very serious.

Using paper methods (tape or punched cards), a

second copy is keyed. If there are any differences from the first copy the reader will jam the keyboard. The inputter then decides which copy is the accurate one.

With magnetic media (tape or disks), a second copy is keyed which is also put on tape or disk unit and the two compared.

With transmitted data, a check is made on **parity bit**, an extra bit added at the preparation stage for each **word**. The check will show if data has been corrupted during transmission.

Very Large-Scale Integration (VLSI) As with **large-scale integration** (LSI) this is a measure of the number of logic **gates** on a single **chip**. Between 1960 and 1970 designers produced more and more logic gates on a single chip, the number approximately doubling every year from the single gate of 1959. First came small-scale integration (SSI) with up to 20 logic gates and then medium-scale integration (MSI) with 20 to 100. By 1969 we had large-scale integration with 100 to 5000 logic gates and since 1975 we have had very large-scale integration with numbers above 5000 on a chip about a half-centimetre square.

Video Conference This is the name given to a discussion between two or more groups of people who are in different places but can see and hear each other. Pictures and sound are carried by the **telecommunication** network and such conferences take place across the world using satellites.

Video Disk   See **Optical Disc**.

Video Signal   In a television set it is this signal that provides the picture though in the case of a television transmission entering through the aerial socket it has to be separated from the sound. Most **microcomputers** will display their **output** on a television set via the aerial socket though for better picture definition one should use a **monitor** which accepts a video signal (this has a lower frequency than the UHF aerial signal). Some video recorders have a composite video output and for this reason many **television receivers** are now being made with video inputs as well as UHF. For the clearest colour picture however the **red, green** and **blue** video signals should be sent separately and this requires both an RGB computer output and an RGB video monitor.

Videotext   The name given to any information service which can display text on the screen of a television set. The code may be transmitted as part of a television picture (**teletext**) or as a coded telephone signal (**viewdata**). A typical page has 24 lines with up to 40 characters per line.

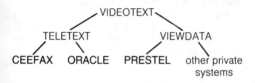

Viewdata An information retrieval service in the form of pages or frames which the user can call up from a dumb terminal or keypad. The pages are transmitted via phone lines from a central computer or direct from the IP (information provider). The

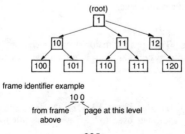

225

information is a structured part of a tree system, each frame having definite well-defined links from the root downwards. Users can access pages by moving up or down a particular pathway from the root, through choices listed on screen and made at the keypad.

Some viewdata services now allow interaction (two-way communication) with users, thus allowing the development of teleshopping, telebanking and booking services.

Virtual Memory   This is a facility available in large modern computers whereby the programmer is not restricted by the size of the machine's memory. The machine translates virtual **locations** that the programmer has specified into actual locations as and when required using **backing stores** to provide the extra memory space.

Virus   The term for major errors which can 'infect' operating systems as a result of the illegal copying of programs or of **bugs**.

Visual Display Unit (VDU)   This is a device, like a television set, used to display the **output** from a computer. It is very similar to a **monitor** except that it is usually associated with a keyboard and is often used as a **terminal** to a computer sometimes from a distance.

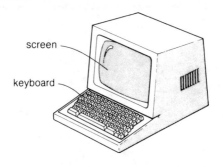

screen

keyboard

VLSI Abbreviation for **Very Large-Scale Integration**.

Voice Input This is the operating of a device controlled by a **microprocessor** not by pressing keys on a keyboard but by speech using a microphone. The device may be mechanical, electrical or electronic. At present machines are able to accept a range of words but these do have to be spoken clearly.

Volatile Memory This refers to all types of **memory** which lose their stored **data** as soon as the power is switched off.

For example: **Core store** and **RAM chips** are volatile whereas magnetic **disk** and **bubble memory** are not.

Wafer The name given to a thin slice cut from a large crystal of germanium or **silicon**. First used in the mid-1950s to make **transistors** which led to the **integrated circuit** or **chip** in 1959. A typical wafer would be 0.01 inch thick, 10 cm in diameter and contain 250 chips.

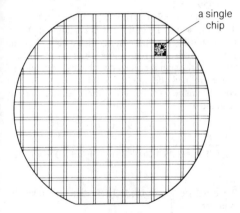

a single chip

Wand Another name for a **light pen**.

Weighted Check Digit This is a method of validating data entry so that mistakes made by the original data collector or while being transferred do not get through. Superior to ordinary **checksum digits**, it is reckoned that hundreds of years would pass before a mistake is wrongly accepted by a computer.

An example of a weighted check digit is the ISBN (International Standard Book Number) of this book: 0 00 459105 4.

The actual number is 0 00 459105, the check digit is 4. When each figure in the number is multiplied by a factor starting from the least significant digit (the digit farthest from the right) and their products are summed, the sum is exactly divisible by a modulus (a predetermined odd number, in this case 11). For the coded number to be valid there should be no remainder.

0	0	0	4	5	9	1	0	5	4
10	9	8	7	6	5	4	3	2	1

$$0 + 0 + 0 + 28 + 30 + 45 + 4 + 0 + 10 + 4 = 121$$

$$121 \div 11 = 11$$

To calculate a weighted check digit, we take the number:

$$0\ 0\ 0\ 4\ 5\ 9\ 1\ 0\ 5\ ?$$

and multiply by the factors from the second digit from the right:

$$
\begin{array}{ccccccccc}
0 & 0 & 0 & 4 & 5 & 9 & 1 & 0 & 5 \\
10 & 9 & 8 & 7 & 6 & 5 & 4 & 3 & 2
\end{array}
$$

and sum their products:

$$0 + 0 + 0 + 28 + 30 + 45 + 4 + 0 + 10 = 117$$

When 117 is divided by 11 there is a remainder of 7. By subtracting 7 from 11, we find the next highest figure which would need to be added to make the sum 117 exactly divisible by the modulus 11:

$$
\begin{aligned}
117 \div 11 &= 10 + \text{remainder } 7 \\
11 - 7 &= 4 \\
4 + 117 &= 121 \text{ (which is exactly divisible by 11)}
\end{aligned}
$$

This is the figure which indicates the check digit, making the complete number 0 00 459105 4.

WIMP   See **Windows Icons Mice Pointers Environment**.

Winchester Disk Drive   Developed in the town of Winchester in the USA, these are designed to take the place of **disk units** for small computers thus avoiding the problems of removing and handling **floppy disks**. These inflexible *hard disks*, as they are also called, behave as a fixed disk system with the read/write head being much closer to the disk. In this way the tracks are much closer together and far more **data** can be stored.

For example: a 5.25-inch Winchester disk could hold a hundred times as much as a normal floppy disk. It would also rotate about ten times faster.

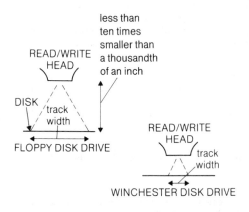

Sizes currently available include 5.25 inches, 8 inches and 14 inches; thus many microcomputer manufacturers offer a choice of Winchester or floppy disk drives with the same machine.

Windows Icons Mice Pointers Environment (WIMP) A set of integrated programs which provide an interface between the user, the operating system, and application programs.

A **mouse**, a small desktop device, is used to move a pointer around the screen. Choices are made by selecting the appropriate icon (pictorial symbol) and clicking the mouse buttons. Icons represent various activities, such as scrap, directory, load, save, and other applications functions. Pull-down menus increase the choices available. Several screen windows

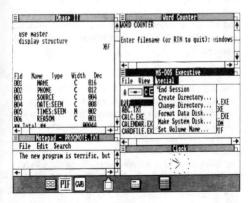

can be displayed, allowing enlargement or reduction within the overall screen-size limits. The WIMP environment largely makes the keyboard redundant for issuing instructions.

Some WIMP programs can allow **multi-tasking**, whereby several programs can be in memory and you can switch between them by using the mouse. A program can be used whilst a previous one is being processed. (In fact, the computer processes a bit of each at a time, but with today's powerful microprocessors, the speed reduction is hardly noticeable.)

Popular WIMP environments include GEM and Microsoft Windows. Many CAD, WP, graphics and desktop publishing applications include WIMP features.

Word The name given to a set of binary digits making up a working group in a particular computer. The **memory** of such a computer is also organized in words, and the 'word length' is measured by the number of **bits** each word contains. 'Word' is generally taken to mean a 16-bit word, an 8-bit word, the most usual in small computers, is called a **byte**, a 32-bit word is called a **double word** and a 64-bit word a *quad*. The longer the word the more quickly the

CPU can work, but longer words require more complex **integrated circuits**.

Most **instructions** that operate the processor contain two parts, an operator (add, subtract) and an **operand** containing the address of the memory **location** to be used. Using a 24-bit word this might be arranged in 8 and 16 bits

★★★★★★★★	★★★★★★★★★★★★★★★★

8 BITS   16 BITS
operator   operand
0-255   0-65535

and could occupy three memory locations in an 8-bit computer or one location in a 24-bit machine.

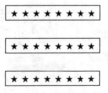

Word Processing (WP) This is the electronic creation of characters, sentences and paragraphs

235

which can be stored, used and changed to produce letters, documents and reports very easily. Word-processing packages have far better features than typewriters. Text can be moved, copied, searched and replaced, and in some cases checked for spelling. Titles can be centred and changes made to a document's layout. Wordwrap (automatic word fit between margins) can be used, as well as justifying text after insertions. Font and print sizes can be altered.

Modern word-processing has WYSIWIG (pronounced wiziwig and meaning What You See Is What You Get) screen features in that text on screen is displayed exactly as it will look when printed on

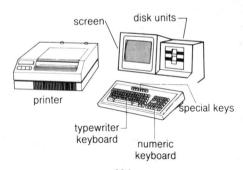

screen — disk units
printer
special keys
typewriter keyboard
numeric keyboard

paper. Word processors can be **mouse**-driven instead of controlled totally from a keyboard. Some manufacturers offer specially designed machines dedicated solely to use as word processors. These often have extra keys to take the place of commands/functions. Popular word-processing packages for ordinary computers include Microsoft Word and Wordstar.

Work Station In today's modern office one sits not just at a desk but at a work station. This has its own **visual display unit** connected to the company's **database** as well as public **viewdata** systems. A keyboard allows the typing of memos and letters which can be sent immediately via the telephone line. Incoming messages are stored so that they can be accepted as required. With such developments the work station does not need to be in an office; it could be on the factory floor or at home.

Work Tape A magnetic tape which is available for use at any time. It might be used to hold the **data** in a sorting **routine** or the intermediate results of a long calculation.

WORM Acronym for Write Once Read Many Times. See **Optical Disc**.

WP   Abbreviation for **Word Processing** or Word Processor.

WYSIWYG   Acronym for What You See Is What You Get, a screen feature used in **word processing**.

Xerographic Laser Printer See **Laser Printer**.

X-Y The two directions of the computer screen or printer output. X represents the horizontal direction and Y the vertical. See also **Plotter**.

X.400 A new **telecommunications** standard which allows computers to talk to each other. See also **Data Communications**.

X-OR Abbreviation for **Exclusive-OR Gate**.

Yell This is what one does when things go wrong. One problem for the **microcomputer** user occurs when the **backing store** (tape or disk) becomes corrupt in some way and it is not possible to load a particular program. It is at this point that the user realises that a **backup** copy was never made let alone the third copy recommended as good practice. Most companies that use a computer are often unaware of how dependent their business becomes on the machine. In fact if their computer system was put out of action completely most would find it difficult to survive. Hence the need for adequate insurance and backup facilities.

Zone This generally refers to specific regions on a **punched card** but can refer to print positions.

For example: in **BASIC**, variables separated by semicolons are printed together whilst those separated by commas are printed in separate zones.

Zone Refining This is the method used to obtain a pure substance such as the **silicon** required for making **integrated circuits**. Starting at one end the material is melted and this molten zone is made to move along the sample to the other end. This is repeated several times always in the same direction and each time more of the impurities move with the molten zone to one end of the sample. In the case of silicon this pure substance is doped and then grown into a large cylindrical crystal (using a **seed crystal**) from which **wafers** are sliced.

Abbreviations and Acronyms

A

A/D	Analogue to Digital
ADA	A programming language
ADC	Analogue-digital converter
ALGOL	ALGOrithmic Language
ALU	Arithmetic Logic Unit
AND	A Logic Gate
APL	A Programming Language
ASCII	American Standard Code for Information Interchange
ATM	Automated Telling Machine

B

BASIC	Beginner's All-purpose Symbolic Instruction Code
BCD	Binary Coded Decimal
BCS	British Computer Society,
BIT	Binary DigIT
BLAISE	British Library Automated Information Service
BSI	British Standards Institute

C

C	A high-level language
CAA	Computer Aided Administration
CAD	Computer Aided Design
CAL	Computer Assisted Learning
CAM	Computer Aided Manufacture
CBT	Computer Based Training
CD-I	Compact Disc Interactive
CD-Rom	Compact Disc Read Only Memory
CIM	Computer Integrated Manufacture
CM	Central Memory
CML	Computer Managed Learning
CMOS	Complementary Metal Oxide Semiconductor
COBOL	Common Business Oriented Language
COM	Computer Output on Microfilm
COMAL	High-level programming language
CORAL	High-level programming language
CP/M	Control Program for Microcomputer
CPS	Characters Per Second
CPU	Central Processing Unit

D

DOS	Disk Operating System
DP	Data Processing
DTL	Diode Transistor Logic
DTP	Desk Top Publishing

E

EAROM	Electrically Alterable ROM
EBCDIC	Extended Binary Coded Decimal Interchange Code
ECMA	European Computer Manufacturers' Association
EDI	Electronic Data Interchange
EFTPOS	Electronic Funds Transfer at Point Of Sale
ELSI	Extra Large Scale Integration
EPROM	Erasable Programmable Read Only Memory

F

FET	Field Effect Transistor
FORTRAN	FORmula TRANslation
4GL	Fourth Generation Language

G H

GIGO	Garbage In Garbage Out
GB	Gigabyte (1000 megabytes)
HZ	Hertz

I

IAL	International Algebraic Language
IAR	Instruction Address Register
IAS	Immediate Access Store
IBM	International Business Machines
IC	Integrated Circuit
ICL	International Computers Limited
IEE	Institute of Electrical Engineers
IEEE	A standard interface
IFIP	International Federation for Information Processing
INTELSAT	INternational TELecommunications SATellite consortium
I/O	Input and Output
IP	Information Provider
ISBN	International Standard Book Number
ISO	International Organization for Standardization
IV	Interactive video

J K

JCL	Job Control Language
K	Kilo
Kbytes	Kilobytes

L

LCD	Liquid Crystal Display
LED	Light Emitting Diode
LOGO	A high-level language
LPM	Lines Per Minute
LSI	Large Scale Integration

M

MAP	Microprocessor Application Project
MB	megabyte
MICR	Magnetic Ink Character Recognition
MIPS	Millions Instructions Per Second
MISP	Microelectronics Industry Support Programme
MODEM	Modulator-Demodulator
MPU	Microprocessor Unit
MS-DOS	Microsoft Disk Operating System

N O

NAND	A Not AND Logic Gate
NCC	National Computing Centre
NEQ	A Non-Equivalence Logic Gate
NLQ	Near Letter Quality
NOR	A Not OR Logic Gate
NOT	A Logic Gate
OA	Office Automation
OCR	Optical Character Recognition
OR	A Logic Gate
OSI	Open Systems Interconnection

P

PASCAL	High-level programming language
PC	Personal Computer
PCB	Printed Circuit Board
PC-DOS	Personal Computer Disk Operating System
PICK	A new operating system
PIXEL	PICture ELements
PILOT	An author language
PIO	Programmable Input/Output
PL/1	Programming Language 1
PLATO	A CBL system
POS	Point Of Sale (terminal)
PROM	Programmable Read Only Memory

Q R

QWERTY	The normal typewriter keyboard
RAM	Random Access Memory
RF	Radio Frequency
RGB	Red, Green, Blue
RJE	Remote Job Entry
ROM	Read Only Memory
RS232	A standard serial interface
RS423	A standard serial interface

S T

SSI	Small Scale Integration
TB	Tetrabyte (1000 gigabytes)
3GL	Third Generation language
TTL	Transistor Transistor Logic
2GL	Second Generation language

U

UHF	Ultra High Frequency
ULA	Uncommitted Logic Array
UNIX	A new operating system

V

VDU	Visual Display Unit
VHF	Very High Frequency
VLF	Very Low Frequency
VLSI	Very Large Scale Integration

W

WIMP	Windows, Icons, Mice, Pointer
WORM	Write Once Read Many (times)
WP	Word Processor
WYSIWYG	What You See Is What You Get

X

X-Y	Two directions at right angles
X.400	New telecommunication standard
XOR	Exclusive-OR logic gate